"I loved this book! It's quirky. It's pleasantly irreverent. It's heartfelt and faithful. Much like Beth herself! Thank you, Beth, for encouraging us all to drop the labels that keep us from knowing who we really are in Christ!"

—BRIAN SPAHR, Executive Pastor, Come2Go Ministries

"Beth's energy and authenticity are front-and-center in all that she does. She is a woman who is willing to ask—and attempt to answer—even the toughest questions. From her faith, to cancer, to managing a career and being a mom, Beth embodies the spirit of strength and forgiveness. That inspirational spirit jumps off the pages in this funny, heartwarming book."

—MEREDITH BRONK, President & CEO, OST

"The second act in any story is where the main character gets in over his or her head, is pushed to innovate, to move forward in faith, to live free from who others expect them to be. In *Remorseless*, Beth's transparency and honesty leads readers deeper to escape the labels, guilt, and barriers stopping them from becoming who God intended them to be. Turning the pages of Beth's story, oftentimes laughing and crying out loud, you'll find yourself with a renewed hope no matter the adversity that stands before you and rediscover your story has a greater purpose."

—DEREK WILLIAMS, executive producer and director of over 500 episodes of unscripted television syndicated on over 60 channels worldwide, and co-author of *Street Smarts from Proverbs*

"Beth Fisher's book *Remorseless* is both relatable and thought provoking. It will inspire readers to show up and be who they were meant to be even in the face of adversity."

—A<small>ILEEN</small> W<small>EINTRAUB</small>, Best-selling author of *Never Too Young! 50 Unstoppable Kids Who Made a Difference*

"Beth's transparency and vulnerability are a breath of fresh air. I found myself laughing out loud one minute, and soul-searching the next. With God's help, Beth has chosen to live beyond the labels assigned to her by others. You can too! If you're still trying to figure out who you really are, this is a great place to start."

—B<small>RUCE</small> W. M<small>ARTIN</small>, author of *Desperate For Hope*

"Gaining insight through tough, sometimes rough, experiences, Beth shares her story and newfound wisdom in a fresh, real way. Beautifully crafted, these are words that everyone needs to hear."

—K<small>IM</small> S<small>ORRELLE</small>, Executive Director of Rays of Hope International

"We absolutely loved this book—this story—this journey. We really don't know if any words we could say can do *Remorseless* the justice it deserves. Immediately, we identified with Beth's pain and inner conflict, especially in light of her insatiable zest and positivity towards life. We understood her questioning and confusion. A wonderful communicator and writer, Beth makes you *feel* experiences, not just read about them. We loved *Remorseless* for its vulnerability, honesty, the *Remorseless Reminders* at the end of each chapter, and the faith struggles and wisdom that were learned and shared. I highly recommend this book to everyone who has experienced life's struggles—which pretty much includes all of us. We all need to know that we are not alone in our experience."

—Dave Dravecky (Former Major League Pitcher for the SF Giants) and Jan Dravecky, Authors of *When You Can't Comeback* and *Do Not Lose Heart*

"Reading Beth Fisher's powerful and inspiring book *Remorseless* is like sitting down for a long overdue heart-to-heart with that one true friend who you can always trust to tell you like it is, like it's needed to be heard; and, because this friend has lived a life worth living (and has all the tee-shirts to prove it), you can also trust that what shall be told and what shall be heard shall always come from a place of love and a keen sense of understanding."

—Kurt Brindley, Leukemia/GVHD survivor and author of *How Not To Die: In 13 Easy Steps*

"Beth Fisher speaks from the heart and that's what makes this book such a fascinating read. Her powerful stories are delivered with such emotion that it makes you feel like you've known her forever. She doesn't accept labels, assumptions or expectations from others, but finds comfort with who she is in the sight of God. Her main point is clear—you are perfect and acceptable the way God made you and above all, you are loved. You will enjoy *Remorseless* and will be able to relate to Beth as she takes you on a one-of-a-kind journey. Hunker down for a unique ride."

—Del Duduit, Best-selling and award-winning author

"Beth Fisher authentically shares compelling stories from her life to help each of us discover our true identity. She provides deep insights into the heart of our Creator, who desires to free us from the prison of viewing life through our clouded perspective and the limited assumptions of others. *Remorseless* empowers us with the crystal clear 20/20 vision of God in Jesus Christ in order to fully engage with His incomparable love."

—**Mitch Kruse**, host of *The Restoration Road with Mitch Kruse* and author of *Restoration Road* and *Street Smarts from Proverbs*

"Regret and remorse keeps too many of us imprisoned, helpless to free ourselves from the past and enjoy lives of daily peace. In *Remorseless*, Beth Fisher's gutsy transparency lets us know she not only understands, but cares. By sharing dramatic elements of her true story, she shows us what it's like to pull yourself out of an abyss and fully embrace who you are. The *Remorseless Reminders* at the end of each chapter are great, providing a fresh dose of perspective or an emotional lift when you need them. Equal parts practical and inspirational, *Remorseless* is a great read!"

—**Anita Agers-Brooks**, international speaker, business/life coach, and award-winning author of *Getting Through What You Can't Get Over* and other books

REMORSELESS

*Learning to Lose Labels,
Expectations, and Assumptions—
Without Losing Yourself*

BETH FISHER

Copyright © 2020

**Remorseless:
Learning to Lose Labels,
Expectations, and Assumptions—
Without Losing Yourself**

Beth Fisher

Brookstone Publishing Group
P.O. Box 211, Evington, VA 24550
BrookstoneCreativeGroup.com

Ordering Information:
Special discounts are available on quantity purchases by corporations, associations, and others. For details, contact Brookstone Publishing Group at the address above.

ISBN: 978-1-949856-23-1 (print), 978-1-949856-24-8 (epub)

To every version of our former selves—the label-less and limitless child from whom each of us grew, and to my daughter, Olivia. May you never stop being who you were created to be on your journey to becoming who you are meant to become.

ACKNOWLEDGMENTS

While there are far too many people than I could even begin to name who have made this book possible, I would be utterly remiss not to mention the following individuals who have been along for the crazy ride.

Thank you, Ryan. As in, Fisher—a last name I never expected to bear. You, sweet husband o'mine, are relentless in your encouragement and continual support. You know more than anyone that while "third time is a charm," it's also work and commitment. Thanks for putting up with me, not giving up, and for using your artist's eyes to help me see things in myself that I was afraid to notice before. I love you.

I am grateful to every single person with whom I grew up in Minerva, Ohio. I will always love John Mellencamp's lyrics (and no, not just because he used to have multiple last names) solely because they are true: *Educated in a small town…taught the fear of Jesus in a small town…No I cannot forget where it is that I come from…I cannot forget the people who love me.*

To my three life-long friends, Becky, Beth, and Chels. No amount of distance, number of hiatuses, unforeseen circumstances, or laundry lists of blackmail-worthy dirt could ever come between us. Thank you for always being there and never letting me forget any of it—including and especially, who I truly am.

To my circle of solid and newfound friends including all my

REMORSELESS

Burn Boot Camp sisters, especially Shannon, Kat, and Simona—thank you for doing mid-life together and making me laugh daily. And to the very first person I crossed a marathon finish line alongside, you were always usually right. Thank you, Foster, for being the second smartest person I know and an unwavering source of understood love and friendship.

I am beyond thankful for the strong group of women who helped me navigate the world of authorship, editing, and publishing. Anita Brooks—you are amazing! Thank you for your wisdom, boldness, frank and accurate honesty, direction, encouragement, support and inspiration. You held me both personally and professionally accountable and somehow managed to never run out of red font! Thank you for your genius editing, guidance, friendship and believing in me.

To my publisher and the entire team at Brookstone Publishing Group—your expertise and dedication to this project not only helped me realize my life dream, but it made this book so much more than I ever imagined it could be. Suzanne Kuhn, you are every positive adjective I have left in my vernacular. From your adroit and interminable knowledge in the book and publishing world, to your authenticity and genuine care and concern for the well-being of others, I learned so much from being in your presence. I am forever grateful and indebted to you.

Thank you to each of my advance readers, commenters, and those who provided this first-time author with an endorsement. I value your efforts and help, without which, I would have been much less steady and resolute.

Ann, my ever-sardonic, witty and priceless friend, you were the impetus for me to finally *write*. Whether it was inspirational or more, "I'll show her!" in response to the day you first met me is

ACKNOWLEDGMENTS

anyone's guess. But please know you had me at hello. And also—the best kind of friends are often the ones who show up on our journeys when we expect them least and need them most. Thank you.

My IOS work compadres, I appreciate you. There's no way I could have written this book without your willingness and graciousness to allow me an extended sabbatical. I realize how rare that is and how lucky I am. Thank you, as well, for being a long-standing and imperative part of my life journey. And no—no discounts for any of you. *I'm still in sales.*

Finally, thank you seems awfully inadequate to my family of origin. Sarah, my little yet way taller sister, thanks for being the you that you are. Thanks for getting your blood taken when I was sick, even though you hate needles, and thanks for not disowning me every time I probably made it reasonable to do so over the last forty-three years.

Mom and Dad, there are neither enough nor adequate words to express how much I love you guys. I can't imagine what my life would have been without you. Someday, when it's time for you to leave this earth, I hope you know the impact you had upon it—especially in the lives of your girls.

May all girls everywhere know that they are unconditionally loved for who they are, too.

FOREWORD

I first met Beth Fisher at a conference for writers and speakers where, apparently, I asked her this pointed question: "What is your question for me?" I confess to not remembering this exact exchange, but do know that I've asked this question numerous times to new writers eager for advice and help.

Beth and I have been asking each other pointed questions ever since. Sometimes there's laughter involved, sometimes tears, sometimes we crack wise and have crummy attitudes. And sometimes we dig into the deep issues of life as we seek answers to our questions.

Remorseless asks a lot of pointed questions, and I can hear Beth's voice throughout. Her ability to cut to the real issues; her humor; her life lessons learned the hard way through experience, hurt, and growth.

Her pithy, wise statements continue to resonate with me long after reading them. Statements like, "No one wants to be confined to a reality that belongs to someone else." And, "Making assumptions about others is human nature, but it's rarely accurate." Plus, "People will treat you how you allow them to."

Strong words from a strong woman. *Remorseless* is a strong book, too. Beth doesn't mince words as she describes her struggles and questions that began in childhood, wend through three marriages and one cancer journey, and end up at the very face of God.

"When your baseline belief is that your thoughts and therefore, you, are not important, it's hard to figure out who you are supposed to be. And when you don't know who you are supposed to be, it's hard to know how to live accordingly," she says. We all feel it, don't we?

Beth takes you through so many of the issues that bog us down as we search for ourselves and God, and she does it with honesty, a sharp wit, and a deep love for you, her reader. She asks, from a heart of deep concern and love, "Do you feel like the real you?"

You will find *Remorseless* to be, well, remorseless as Beth pushes you to defy the labels and find your real self. This book and this journey are worth every effort.

Ann Byle is a professional freelance writer for both local and national publications, including Publishers Weekly. *Author of* Christian Publishing 101, *Ann is owner of AB Writing Services and media specialist for Baker Book House. She endeavors to live and exemplify authenticity.*

CONTENTS

Acknowledgments ix
Foreword xiii
Introduction 1
Chapter 1   Fictitious Labels 7
Chapter 2   Thinly-Veiled Messaging 17
Chapter 3   Know Thyself 27
Chapter 4   Asinine Assumptions 41
Chapter 5   Narrative Loops 51
Chapter 6   Watered-Down Version 63
Chapter 7   Two Sides to Every Coin 73
Chapter 8   Deconstruction 85
Chapter 9   Guilty by Association 95
Chapter 10 Filling in our Unknowns 107
Chapter 11 Process and Preparation 117
Chapter 12 Questioning Disparities 127
Chapter 13 Living In Accordance 139
Chapter 14 Tiresome Transactional Responses 149
Chapter 15 Understanding Root Cause 163
Chapter 16 Unhidden 175
Chapter 17 Giftings 187
Chapter 18 Walk Don't Run 197
Conclusion 207
About the Author 211

INTRODUCTION

Remorseless: Without guilt in spite of wrongdoing.

You are who you are for a reason. Yet there are likely people and situations continually trying to convince you otherwise. Have you ever felt like you were living inauthentically in areas of your life because you caved in to the wrong version of yourself?

This book is meant to offer you real-life insight based on real-life situations. I want to explain how you can go about viewing and tackling your important decisions, transitions, and relationships differently from here on out—based on living a no holds barred, real-you existence, remorselessly.

I spent a lot of time trying to decide how to lay out this book. I spent even more time trying to figure out if I wanted to write it at all. The first part is easier to address, since it's more methodical.

The pages that follow contain transparent and intentional advice on how to make choices in life based on who you truly are. You will read what happens when you don't make decisions based on your authentic self—as I did for many years. Whether you are in a seasonal transition, i.e. heading to college, empty-nesting, divorcing, changing your job, experiencing a physical affliction, or you simply desire to set and exceed a goal, I want to provide relatable and easy to apply insights, so you don't stay stuck in indecision and inaction.

I've been through many difficult situations, as you'll soon discover. Some almost broke me. Because my life has been disordered at times, some of the stories within the following chapters may seem chronologically choppy. The abridged version looks like this: formative years, college (married eight months after graduation), baby (fifteen months later), and divorce (two years later). Then there was cancer (uncovered during the divorce), remarried one month after the divorce was final (I know), and then, married to husband #2 for twelve years. When that marriage ended, I was in my mid-thirties and swore off relationships for good. As of this book's publication date, I've been married for three years, because hey—no one likes a quitter—and remorseless relationships actually do exist. In other words, there's hope, people.

Since I know how hard life can seem, I also want to provide encouragement for those of you who may be thinking, *there is no stinking way I can do this*, or *this cannot be happening right now*, and/or *surely, this isn't my actual life*. Because I've been there, it's important for me to share in a meaningful manner the ways in which I have been able to get through crazy, unforeseen (fine, and some totally seen in advance but I proceeded anyway) obstacles. I know from experience, you can navigate your way back on course.

As one of my all-time favorites, Maya Angelou said, "When you learn, teach. When you get, give."

I learned mostly through the school of *What Were You Thinking?* I grew up in an era where it wasn't proper for our mothers to order pizza on a random weekday, let alone share the details of their private transgressions. Thus, my mom didn't warn me about looming dangers like irrelevant labels or immature boys.

To be clear, I am not a specialist or certified guru with a gaggle of initials after my name. What I am though, is a real, regular, midlife menopausal woman who believes we can do anything we set our

INTRODUCTION

minds to if we have people in our corner. People who come alongside us on our journeys, to mentor, guide, and give us direction so we can avoid the detours ahead. Those who have traveled before us often know better routes to take, so we don't have to end up lost or sidetracked ourselves. I definitely could've used Google Maps back in the day.

I am also someone who learned that I don't know the absolute answer for everybody else. I do know how to get from a little village in northeast Ohio, and a childhood filled with conflict and questions, to becoming a peace-filled woman with answers, and a deep sentimentality for my upbringing. I do know how to go from being an apprehensive young girl, suffocating under the heavy expectations and labels other people cast on me, to a confident and loving woman. I do know how to go from being immobile and isolated, to leaping out of bed each morning ready to take on a new day. I do know how to go from two divorces to a stable marriage filled with unconditional love. I do know how to go from succeeding (by worldly standards) in corporate America, to walking away from it, and feeling stronger as a result. And I positively know how to go from being a reckless complaisant, desperate to be accepted for who I truly am, to a woman who is so filled with gratitude and love for others, for the gifts I've been given, for my passions and relationships, that I no longer chase negative ideals or seek unhealthy approval.

Most importantly though, I know how to go from thinking God was going to send me to Hell ten times a day, to enjoying a confident relationship with him. And not in a label-y "evangelical" sort of way, which leads me to the more difficult part about publishing this book—whether I wanted to write it at all. The pages that follow contain some of the most transparent struggles with the hardest relationship of my life. Christianity. God. Church. Religion. Yada, yada, yada (labels), puke.

You see, I'm not like the standard Christian woman. Even writing that sentence is ridiculous to me, because what does that even mean? Right. That's the point. It shouldn't mean *anything* other than someone who loves Christ. And yet, walk into (most) churches today and unless you look like, act like, and think like everyone else, you're pretty much shunned. Plus, God-forbid, don't question anything you're told, or you'll be left for insignificant on the side of the road you got stuck on.

I didn't always know the way mainstream religion operated—and I still don't fit some of the molds. Up until my mid-thirties, I thought the Bible was alphabetized (it isn't). I grew up Catholic. My belief system was decided many generations ago on my behalf. That is not to say I am unappreciative or disgruntled by growing up "in the faith." Much of my sentimentality and nostalgia stems from the comfort of squeezing into a pew every week during my formative years, and for several thereafter.

I don't know about you, but for me, the frustration of seemingly unsolvable situations makes me tired. I became exhausted by hearing one kind of message but seeing with my own apparently hell-bound eyes, an altogether different reality. People's words and actions did not always align, not to mention, the things I was being taught about God made no sense to me. When you're young, this just seems confusing—as you grow older, it becomes infuriating.

I'd like to tell you that I figured out this disconnect when I stopped going to the Catholic church. I'd like to tell you that I didn't make decisions, consciously or otherwise, based on my fear of letting God down or constantly burning in eternal pain. And I'd really like to tell you that feeling ostracized and abandoned by my

INTRODUCTION

church family hurt less than when it happened within even closer circles. But I can't.

Not only did church challenge my thoughts, but it is also where I learned *who I am*. It's probably where, along with other societal constructs and a zillion presuppositions, many of you learned who you are, too.

So, let me assure you of this—you matter. We all do—regardless of past choices. Somewhere, deep within me—*the real me*—is that same little girl who has now experienced enough relationships to understand, unwaveringly, that there is one worth fighting for. I am convinced that if we saw ourselves as God sees us, we'd avoid so many bad decisions.

The understanding of who we were created to be is paramount. That is why I decided to let go of my insecurities and confidently write this book. Since I am not fluffy, I can promise you nothing you read is going to be spiritually fluffy, either. There is nothing worse than reading hollow rhetoric over and over and coming away with the feeling you simply took on some other kind of label (sinner).

My hope for you is that after journeying with me, you will come away exhaling one giant sigh of relief, along with an affirmation and resurgence of the real YOU.

Believe me—if a stubborn, thrice-married, label-hating, quintessential Catholic girl can be transformed, so can you.

CHAPTER 1

FICTITIOUS LABELS

I'm not a very good Christian. This is just one of many labels I embraced. I often marvel at how many inaccurate identifications I've assigned myself and been assigned by others: ugly, pretty, dumb, smart, fat, annoying, hot, athletic, loud, mouthy, ambitious, driven, bossy, or my personal favorite—a crazy Christian who doesn't put out. That last one was uttered when I was in my late-thirties, recently divorced, by an adult man who was trying to convince his friend to ask me on a date. What made him think that way, I have no idea, but I do wonder whether it was meant to be a compliment or a dig.

I avoided that date like a porta-potty on a hot July day, yet I had far less success avoiding years of appointed labels. Because of this, it breaks my heart and riles me up when I see people *define* themselves based on someone else's erroneous characterizations. It pains me even more when I watch life decisions being made based upon some absurd label given by another flawed and labeled-themselves human being.

It's like a package you receive, open, and can't return, because there's no indication of where the gift came from or how much it will cost to send back. You end up stuck with it. But I can tell you when we receive an ill-fitting label and choose to keep it, the price is great, causing years of wrong decisions and regret. It drives me crazy—because labels do not allow for the beautiful differences and nuances that exist within each individual. Labels can also segregate and alter relationships.

> **❝ LABELS DO NOT ALLOW FOR THE BEAUTIFUL DIFFERENCES AND NUANCES THAT EXIST WITHIN EACH INDIVIDUAL.**

I remember one Christmas morning, when my daughter, Olivia, was not quite three years old. She shimmied over to the brightly-lit tree, grabbed a gift and flung off the wrapping. It was mid-morning. An egg casserole baked in the oven. Christmas music blared. Sweater-adorned family members talked and sang and shouted over one another. As is the case with most split families, this was not the first family celebration Olivia and I attended that season.

Still wearing her furry, red zip-up pajama romper, Olivia shouted, "Mama, look! *Another* pair of roller skates!"

I froze on my way to save the burning casserole.

"Thank you, Aunt Barb. I will put these next to the other pair of skates I got last night," my little girl said.

In the scrambling of opening presents, I was relieved that only my sister-in-law and I heard Olivia's response, my other family members were oblivious.

My daughter has always been a loving and empathetic minimalist. She was sincere, excited, and truly appreciative of the gift. But she was also conflicted, since clearly, one pair of roller skates was enough. Even in that well-intended exchange, the gift could not be returned for fear of hurting someone's feelings.

Later that night, I tucked Liv into bed. She looked up at me and said, "Did I make Aunt Barb mad, Mama?"

FICTITIOUS LABELS

I knew why she was asking.

"No, honey. You didn't make her mad. And you didn't do anything wrong."

"But when I told her I would put my skates next to the other ones, she didn't smile," Olivia said. To this day, my daughter will tell you she feels trepidation when she opens gifts.

Just like receiving the same gift twice, when we take on a label that God didn't intend for us, our future responses and outlooks change. But there is one gift I've come to believe every human being on the planet shares—we are infinitely valuable. We are all created with equal worth. You haven't messed up so much that your pricelessness is diminished. Regardless of what you have said to yourself or someone else has told you, apart from any label placed on you, your packaging is not flawed.

I often come from a place of great passion in my wording. *Feisty* and *intense* are also labels I've been given over the years. Yet, along with *passionate*, these labels are two I refuse to return. Over the years, many people have tried to get me to—that's for sure. On more than one occasion, different individuals (of the male variety) told me they *loved my feisty and intense* personality. I heard those words as affirmation, early on in our getting-to-know-you relationship phase. However, as time and the relationship progressed, the same individuals told me they *hated my feisty and intense personality*. The messaging confused me. I didn't understand how identical words could be used to mean something so vastly different when I was the same person.

Thus, I am *passionate* about the pitfalls of labeling. I have experienced immense pain succumbing to a discounted version of myself. I know all too well how deeply improper labels can damage and baffle us. Instead of moving us toward a limitless life based on who we were created to be, incorrect labeling can get us stuck and off course. While that is all true—I had to learn to take accountability for my mindset—clear perspective is a two-way street.

> **I DIDN'T UNDERSTAND HOW IDENTICAL WORDS COULD BE USED TO MEAN SOMETHING SO VASTLY DIFFERENT WHEN I WAS THE SAME PERSON.**

In the past, I too, have placed inaccurate labels on others. I've unintentionally made people feel badly about themselves, without understanding what I was doing or how it was happening.

For all the things people call us—how do we know what to believe? How do we know what is true? What happens when we make decisions based on wrong beliefs? How do we learn to make choices that aren't based on lies about ourselves?

For an insatiably curious girl, these questions, along with bad decisions, wrong relationships, and remorse haunted me most of my life. I was ashamed of my own story—until life interrupted my carefully constructed script. I went from living in response to what others labeled and expected of me, to facing a crisis that left me stripped of my very DNA. And let me tell you, I didn't see that coming. But I'm getting ahead of myself.

I found two things crucial in my transformative journey. The first was mustering the courage to forgive. I had to forgive myself for the bad choices I made while living according to assigned labels. For too long, I believed the labels. I made life-altering decisions based on them.

The second part in my transformative journey came from another label—a name—God. How I approached God and how

I thought He approached me during times of distress is probably not what you're used to hearing. I'm kind of an "in your face meets empathetic" person—except I was never sure how to be in your face and reverent at the same time. Today, I finally make no apologies for who I am, the labels I've been given, or my relationship with God. I have become unshakable in my belief that not only is it useless to label humans—but trying to do so with God is even more counterproductive.

I used to get so annoyed—and shockingly if you knew me—speechless, when someone branded me with a word or phrase. *You're so 'in your face.'* Yes, I am. *You're so empathetic.* Yes, I am.

For me, that's the problem and shallowness of labels. I can be both. But I am *more* than just those descriptors. *I am complex.*

So, if human beings are more—way more—than words alone can convey, how in the world are we comfortable with labeling *God?*

After a long haul in personal experience, churches, and accredited studies in divinity, I no longer label God. Whether you use capital *Him,* lower-case *his,* capital *Her,* lower-case *she,* the *Creator,* the *Divine, Father,* go on with the list—I don't think it matters. God transcends gender, space, time, humanness and platitudes. He showed up in the world with a bunch of people whom He created and loves, so I know he understands our identification struggle.

Nothing summed up my conviction of this more than my kind and loving grandmother, Rita. Years ago, when she was still alive, I heard my mom speaking to her on the phone one day, as they did every Thursday morning. I waited for them to hang up before I asked a pressing question.

"Mom, why do you call Gram by her first name? You call her *Rita* instead of *Mom.*"

She smiled.

"I always have, honey," she said. "Your gram told me it's not *what* you call someone, but *how* you say it. It's about the love and respect behind the name, not the name itself."

That made sense to me. Once I believed it was okay to refer to God as I understood God to be, I stopped referring to myself differently than I understood myself to be. In doing so, I began to feel more genuine and non-fictitious than ever. It just took me a while to roll out the red carpet, throw my hands up and say to my true self, "Hey, welcome to the party. Glad you could finally make it!"

66 IT'S ABOUT THE LOVE AND RESPECT BEHIND THE NAME, NOT THE NAME ITSELF.

Forgiving God for what I believed to be His bad behavior was an integral part of learning to understand myself. This has unfolded in ways which still make me laugh in disbelief. I had to unravel and deconstruct many of the labels and expectations I had been taught about God as part of my traditional church upbringing. And yes, I eventually realized God did not need my forgiveness.

I remember the first time my mom dropped me off at the rectory, which I later learned was another name for house. Our priest lived in the rectory, along with Anna—who I think was the equivalent of a house mom in a sorority, but no one ever told me for sure.

The door opened immediately after I rang the bell. "Hi, Beth," Anna said. "Come on in. God is waiting for you."

I was six years old. My highly pragmatic, literal black-and-white thinking was solidly intact before I even crawled. Thus, scared as I was, I stood on the floral rug in the entryway of the rectory and refused to move.

"Beth, follow me," Anna said.

"No, thank you," I said.

My feet were anchored like the Titanic at the bottom of the ocean.

After Anna cajoled, bartered, and begged me to hold her soft and wrinkly hand, I walked into the living room with my eyes closed. Without dropping Anna's grip, I slowly relaxed my eyes open, one squeezed slit at a time.

"Well, hello there," a clean-shaven middle-aged man with a full head of pitch-black hair smiled at me from behind a newspaper, as he lounged in a leather recliner.

"Why does God look like that?" I whispered to Anna. I didn't yet know his name was Father Mike.

I don't remember the words Anna spoke to assuage my fear, but after the encounter, I remained confused for many years about how religion and relationship should look. This limiting belief cost me a lot of energy and time.

Showing up in my own story required me to stop running from the Creator and my true self. I had to be in real relationship—with both a God I had all wrong, and a girl I'd been taught not to like so much. For someone who used to be capital T—*terrible* at relationships, it was no easy feat.

> **SHOWING UP IN MY OWN STORY REQUIRED ME TO STOP RUNNING FROM THE CREATOR AND MY TRUE SELF.**

Life and its constant education, situations I didn't see coming let alone plan for, and all the brokenness resulting from bad choices, were my main teachers for many years. Those were not my favorite classes. I didn't learn much, other than life was hard, unfair, and often didn't make much sense. And yes, there were moments I wondered aloud, "What's the point?"

Today I can tell you.

All of the areas of growth and transformation in my life happened not only when I least expected it, but audaciously, while not on my To-Do List. A consummate planner (i.e. former control freak), I had my entire life planned out by the time I was in seventh grade. It was written out and itemized in red gel pen. I hung it on my paneled bedroom wall, so I'd be sure to see it daily and stay on course. Goals. Plans. Dreams. Direction.

None of it happened.

What did happen was pretty much the inverse of everything I had conjured up for my life. And while I didn't know who or what to blame for my failed strategy, I can look back today and see the commonalities between why I wanted each goal/decision/effort to happen in the first place. This lack of understanding about *who I truly am*—as well as who our Creator created me to be—impacted everything.

(Newsflash in case you're pressed for time and want the Cliff Notes version: the problem was never the labels).

Once I recognized the correlation between how I went about life and how I viewed God (and therefore, myself) during the various stages and seasons of life, I started to come to terms with the following:

1. The ways and whys behind my decision-making.

2. The action or inaction I endeavored as part of my daily existence and during times of trial.

3. How I showed up in relationship—both intimate and worldly ones.

This is my hope for you: introspection, growth, change, and letting go of a whole lot of blame and frustration. Sure, it's always way more fun to say, "Seriously—do you remember when you went out with the guy who showed up at your door wearing a shark's tooth necklace and not much else? No wonder things didn't work out."

But fun and easy can only get us so far.

REMORSELESS REMINDERS

- Labeling segregates and alters relationships.

- Everyone is the same—equally valuable and also equally branded.

- Forgiveness for bad choices that were made while living a false version of yourself is necessary in order to move forward.

- God and humans are too immeasurably complex to be defined by the limiting nature of labels. Words alone are inadequate descriptors.

CHAPTER 2

THINLY-VEILED MESSAGING

Our modern-day generation may beg to differ that fun and easy only gets people so far. Instant gratification, immediate validation, and uncomplicated daily lives are what many individuals not only prefer—it's what they are used to. I think we need a cultural overhaul.

"I love life," and, "Life is messed up," both represent how the world presently operates.

This or that. Us or them. Black or white. Left or right. Rich or poor. Men or women. Gay or straight. Baby boomers or millennials. Right or wrong. Can we at least agree that the "my way" versus "your way" mentality isn't doing anything other than making our heads hurt? And can we please agree, it's not helpful?

Labeling is not useful to humans in any capacity. Nor is rigid, controlling, two-choice-only thinking, whether conveyed via direct Twitter rants—or passive-aggressive, indirect insults. Sometimes, don't you just want to say to your mom, "As much as you beat around the bush, you could open up a landscaping company?"

No matter the delivery, labeling is destructive.

"You're so beautiful." The first time I heard these words, I loved them.

It was 1978 and I was in kindergarten when I felt a gentle tap on the back. Mrs. Forrester, my first formal teacher, handed me a book and simultaneously complimented me with her heart-felt expression for no other reason than I was *me*. Her warm smile, soft touch, and bright blue eyes told me she meant what she said. I believed her words—I believed her.

The second time I heard, "You're so beautiful," I was thirteen and believed the statement a little less.

His actions—his demeanor—did not match his words. He wanted something. His motives were not as pure as Mrs. Forrester's had been. I was too young to fully understand the difference between pure messages and those you must filter through. Today, all we've got to do is log onto social media and see example after example, as people become the stars of their own movies—many of which are fiction.

> **FICTITIOUS LABELS DO NOT LEAD TO AUTHENTIC LIVING—INSTEAD, THEY MISDIRECT, MISGUIDE, AND MOVE US FURTHER AWAY FROM WHO WE WERE CREATED TO BE.**

What you see online is not always the most authentic version of one's self. Someone needs to rewrite the scripts we're reading from, because the discrepancy between the actual truth and counterfeit postings prove we are a mess. How many times have you thought less about yourself, your partner, or your kids after scrolling through pictures on social media? Even one time is too many. Just because we label ourselves blissful, carefree, or loving, does not make what really goes on in our lives, fact. Nor does convincing ourselves that lies are truth help us proactively deal with situations that need addressed. Many times, when we buy into other people's inauthentic stories, we avoid showing up in our own. Fictitious labels do not lead to authentic living—instead, they misdirect, misguide, and move us further away from who we were created to be.

God bless you? Easily said. But God blessing strangers? Someone different from us? Someone who makes us uncomfortable because they are not wearing the right label? How about God bless *all* people. Like that cripple, what's his face? The kid with the limp? What's his name? Oh, that's right, Tiny Tim. *God bless us everyone.*

Wait, did that make you uncomfortable? The "cripple" part? If so, good. Because I need your full attention so we can move on to ditching inappropriate labels and getting back on course. And I'm just getting warmed up. If you're not uncomfortable, then you'll likely understand why I feel so strongly about what I'm going to say next.

Assigning false labels can lead to a drifting entitlement and graceless disorder that I firmly believe serve as the impetus for society's self-destruction. Social media platforms have done a tremendous job of controlled labeling. Despite fictitious, thinly-veiled "Look at me! I'm so great and you're such a loser!" messaging, social media is also at times, serving decent purposes. Things like crowdfunding pages for those in need and missing children APB's provide messages intended to serve others. But when both the originator and intent of the message are self-serving, social media often becomes a giant time-sucking vat of kerosene which tauntingly soaks people's lonely and aching bodies in its toxic fumes. The scene is set for a final strike of the match to engulf us in the flames of botched behaviors. From identity crises to divides as insufferable as racism—people's actions deteriorate in public forums.

We know social media is a slippery slope, and yet we continue to log-in daily, sometimes even hourly or more. For some people, online viewing causes ongoing tumult and downward spiraling. It can stoke emotional fires, but still leaves us feeling cold inside.

In complete transparency, I confess I am not immune. Just yesterday, I scrolled through my Facebook newsfeed and saw a post which purported to have the answer to a loving, successful marriage. You know, the kind of advice that was filled with so much ooey gooey obviousness, it would have thrown anyone into a sugar induced coma.

Spend quality time together, schedule a "date day," then display pictures of the two of you in the sun making shadow hearts. Follow with a nightcap, clinking two Dairy Queen Blizzards™ you are about to consume and presumably spoon feed each other on the couch.

The visual was way too syrupy for me. I could not log off fast enough. And I assure you, it had nothing to do with the individuals themselves or the idea of a happy marriage—I am a fan of both.

I'm on the side of *humankind*. Every single test I've ever taken has rightly concluded that I am "highly extroverted," meaning I'm energized, not depleted, by being around other people. I don't know any strangers, because to me, no one is strange. Everyone is unique and beautiful and broken all in one intentionally created package. Each time I meet someone new, I want to hear *their* story. I want to know what inspires them. Who and what do they love? Why? I want to listen and *really hear* whether they feel like they're seen or heard for who they are. Sadly, few I talk with feel like that occurs.

Last week I volunteered at a local high school for a reverse job-shadow program. I parked in the visitor's lot, hurried into the large, newly constructed steel building and signed in at the office. A jubilant teenager led me to the classroom where I spent four hours of my day. Never one to follow rules, I explained to the rowdy group of eighteen students that we would just talk instead of following any curriculum, and I would fill them in on business processes when we got around to it.

"Who in here knows what they want to do for a living?" I said.

No hands went up. I didn't know if they thought I was boring or uninteresting, or if they were really responding.

"Okay, then maybe you can answer this for me. Who in here feels like they matter, like you are heard and seen for you for who you truly are?" I said.

Eighteen kids snickered.

"What's funny?" I said.

A down-trodden girl sitting in the front row looked up at me and said, "No one ever sees us. People just boss us around based on what they think we should be doing. No one really *knows* who we are."

I looked around the room. Seventeen teenage heads nodded in agreement. As a mom, as an adult, as a *human being*—my heart sank.

At times, societal pressures and social media make us question if we are consequential in any way. It can also make us wonder if others know things we don't. Do other people understand everything about everything and have life figured out, while we cower in our uncertainties, pretending to be someone we are not?

Our human selves can't help but wonder if somebody else has all the answers to living an unblemished and admirable life. Meanwhile, we have no clue. This can cause us to question our own worth and value, and also ask, "Why do some people think everyone else wants to constantly hear what they have to say?"

For a variety of reasons, perhaps including exasperation or impatience, we close our ears and shut down. Yet, all the while, we continue to scroll, read, see, and oftentimes, inexplicably—*believe* the facade.

Where is our discernment? Why have we stopped questioning fact versus fiction? Why have we stopped feeling like we matter and believing we are worth more than what we see displayed on a screen? Discernment protects us from placing fictitious labels on ourselves and others.

We don't know if the Facebook posting "look at us!" married couple argued nine out of the ten hours they spent together on their day date. Maybe they truly are starry-eyed over each other after all this time, and if so, I am thrilled. But I've known far more people who've decided to author their own fictitious accounts by posting about their boring-as-all-get-out-to-me "beautiful day date," then informing the rest of us on how to live a more fulfilling life. Please.

> **DISCERNMENT PROTECTS US FROM PLACING FICTITIOUS LABELS ON OURSELVES AND OTHERS.**

What shocked me even more than the umpteenth puke-inducing post I saw the other day, was other people's comments about it. *You two are the sweetest! Thank you for the advice! My spouse and I need to do this!*

It made me wonder, do twenty-first century, married couples seriously need to be told that one of the best ways to strengthen their relationship is by spending time together? Are we spread so thin that we can't figure this out on our own?

Those of us with parents who grew up in the 60's era of free love, yet surely didn't have sex after we were born, seemed to figure out the "connect by spending time together" formula for a successful marriage—pre-internet. Likewise, their parents before them, and those super old, sexless great-grandparents from the generation before, did too. It's not rocket science. Other people don't need or want to know everything we think, nor are we always in the best position to speak into other people's lives.

What makes us so extraordinary that we believe we're experts on all things, and as such, have earned the right to enlighten everyone else? Our access to social media and more technology than at any prior point in history does not mean the entire Facebook population holds a PhD in the topic du jour.

We just like to believe we do.

The obvious question is, if we really do have all the answers, then why are we such a mess?

The less obvious question is, what if messiness is just one more useless label keeping us off course?

At some point on our individual journeys, we begin to listen to contradicting narratives about ourselves that stem from fictitious labels. While we know these label-y adjectives are neither correct nor indicative of who we truly are, they still seem to stick to us like a bad spray tan. No matter how many weights we lift to gain strength—we can't yank them off.

> **THE LESS OBVIOUS QUESTION IS, WHAT IF MESSINESS IS JUST ONE MORE USELESS LABEL KEEPING US OFF COURSE?**

Thus, we begin to believe. We begin to answer to them. We fail to show up in our authentic stories, because you guessed it— we're committed to acting like we're someone we are not. We create caricatures of ourselves and miss out on a future full of real potentials and possibilities.

Here's the thing, our individual worth plummets over time, after we have tried valiantly to ditch ridiculous mis-matched nametags that were never meant for us in the first place. Over time, we question whether it's just easier and less messy to leave the nametags untouched. Eventually we get tired. We are exhausted by the non-stop questioning going on inside our heads. We get sick of trying to remove the labels ourselves. And we become even more weary after trying to convince others we are not what they say we are.

I've learned that labels are, or at least become at some point in our lives, loosely synonymous with expectations. There is no way to keep the association from happening.

However, there is a deliberate way to release ourselves from this pervasive obstacle. The rub is that labels and expectations are not brief and casual events. Separating ourselves from them takes time and is often a brutal, though necessary, process.

Because I have always been curious and unable to sit still, people labeled me as "such a go-getter" from a very early age. I do not disagree that in the general scheme of things, this is true of my nature. However, it is not *always* true.

When we are labeled in any capacity, one of two things occur—we will either try to live up to the expectation or resist it altogether. We cannot unhear the label—the expectation. It remains in the back of our minds perpetually. Whether we spend our days chasing down a designated nametag like a bunch of papers trapped in a wind tunnel, or curl up on the couch in the fetal position waving a giant, "No thanks, I'm out," white flag—we will confront assigned labels by way of our future actions.

I am good friends with two sisters who shared with me that,

from a very early age, their parents ingrained a belief system into them. They were repeatedly told that they could not say or think they excelled at anything, because other people would perceive them to be egotistical and superior. The fact of the matter is, they are both gifted at many things, including, you know, just being human. However, now into their mid-forties, they each responded to that assigned expectation differently. One sister continues to post photos, news articles, and personal accolades non-stop, while the other is afraid to admit she is good at anything. She hides her God-given talents, and her true self.

> **WHEN WE ARE LABELED IN ANY CAPACITY, ONE OF TWO THINGS OCCUR—WE WILL EITHER TRY TO LIVE UP TO THE EXPECTATION OR RESIST IT ALTOGETHER.**

Make no mistake. Whatever label was wrongly assigned to you produces exactly the expectation you have been trying to defy ever since.

Inaccurate labels left me feeling stuck and inauthentic. They held me back and became my mode of operation, which was fine for a while, as long as I could hide in some form of activity. But the second I took that into *relationship*, my life became a nightmare.

REMORSELESS REMINDERS

- My way versus your way leads to hurtful dichotomies and injustices.

- Labeling is unhelpful, especially in relationships, and is often untrustworthy.

- Discernment skills protect us from placing fictitious descriptors on ourselves and others.

- Other people don't need or want to know everything we think, nor are we always in the best position to speak into other people's lives.

- Our future actions and decisions hang in the balance when we believe made-up labels about ourselves.

CHAPTER 3

KNOW THYSELF

While I am a person who never takes no for an answer, tackles a list like a linebacker, overcomes what other people call adversity on a continual basis, abhors laziness, refuses to believe anything is impossible, and creates more calendars than a lunch lady's cafeteria meal plan—the thought of writing a book has rendered me paralyzed for as long as I can remember. And I can remember everything. (One of many decidedly mixed blessings.)

In paradoxical fashion, I have *always* wanted to be a writer. In no particular order, I also wanted to be: an Olympian, a musician, a lawyer, a librarian, a boxer, a Supreme Court Justice, an actress, a human-rights activist, an eighteen-wheel truck driver, and oh, the president. I always preferred Eleanor over Franklin.

Everything interests me. Sameness bores me. I've yet to find something I don't want to try, and if I'm honest, not thought at least initially, that I would be unable to do.

Let me pause here for a second and say—I get it. As you were reading that list, I'll bet a part of you was thinking, *Who does she think she is?* And as you continued to read on, when I told you in total transparency that I refused to believe I could be stopped from achieving those dreams, you may have thought again, with even more emphatic nausea—*Seriously, who in the heck does she think she is? I don't like her. Get over yourself, woman.*

Trust me—I understand.

Those responses have been crushing me my entire life. Which is exactly why I care so deeply about people. My heart aches for anyone who is not *known or seen for who they truly are*.

Hiding is exhausting. It takes a toll and in some cases a lifetime, to seek your real self.

I can't tell you why I wanted to grow up and try those professions, nor can I tell you why I had any inkling that I might be able to become an actual Olympian. I didn't know the rules or requirements of an Olympian any more than I did a librarian. I only knew that other people worked hard in those professions and looked happy as they were doing so. As I got older, I realized my assessment was not the full picture of how they felt as they performed those tasks or carried out their job functions. They may or may not have been happy in the middle of the process, but they always looked satisfied after they crossed the finish line, job well done.

As I continued to be enamored with those kinds of careers, I recognized some commonalities. Boxers and Olympians and actresses competed and received awards. Lawyers, justices, and librarians got to read books and debate content. I identified human rights activists and strong presidents (or first ladies) as people who affected change to better the lives of others. And obviously, rocking out on the highway always seemed like a good idea—hence, my attraction to becoming a musician or truck driver.

The point is, I knew me. I knew who I was. I knew who I was created to be. I think many of us have a deep sense of that certitude of self from a very young age—it's just that sometimes inaccurate judgments and subsequent false labels can steer us sharply off course.

Even though I love the satisfaction that comes with checking goals off a list, I altered my dream list before I even gave it a chance. Nothing squashes a dream faster than a label.

Who does she think she is? I used to let everyone else be the judge of that.

There is no question fictitious labels are dangerous, but not all labels are harmful. The closer they are to our inner wiring, the more inspired we feel and the less faulty our decisions. Out of all the other titles I tried on, writer was the right fit.

> **NOTHING SQUASHES A DREAM FASTER THAN A LABEL.**

This fact was both substantiated and confirmed for me in 1985 at *Back to School Night* in Mr. Barton's seventh-grade classroom. Upon shaking my parents' hands, he said, "Your daughter is such a pretty writer."

My mom, rocking a navy cable-knit sweater with a crisp, popped-up white collar underneath and a pair of maroon penny loafers, grabbed my arm and silenced me. I knew what she was thinking. *Don't bother correcting his adjective choice, dear.*

Why I had to be silent was the real brain-twister.

The impoverished Appalachian area I lived in was our normal—although I didn't always feel like I fit in.

We were far from wealthy, but my dad had worked very hard and progressed to a white-collar job. Some of the men in our community wore uniforms with name-embroidered patches on their left chests, while my dad's position called for a suit and tie. It didn't take too many mean-spirited taunts for me to understand that my father's long days and nights, toiling to educate himself around his work hours, contributed to why I sometimes felt singled-out. It took many years before I appreciated that he was merely dressed in another style of uniform worn by hard-working professionals, and what it took for him to earn his suit and tie.

My parents had neither much money nor experience when they married—my mom at twenty and my dad twenty-three. I was born less than a year later. I'm pretty sure they did more than sleep in the back seat of a giant Oldsmobile during their two-day honeymoon at Niagara Falls.

Once married, my dad worked in a factory during the day and played guitar in bands at night to put food on the table and soon enough, formula in a bottle. Realizing his intellect could take him beyond the plant, he became more than just a mandatory union member. At twenty-six, he was voted in as the union president. Maybe Eleanor and Franklin weren't the best presidential role models after all.

My two-year-old self clearly had no idea how Dad felt about his position of perceived authority as a union president. But later, my teenaged-self better understood Dad's thinking.

One night, as he stabbed his piece of City Chicken, a fake-ish piece of meat on a popsicle stick popular in our Ohio area, Dad said, "Collective bargaining? Why don't they 'collectively' do their jobs?" Quickly, he took a bite from some of the starch, vegetable and obligatory roll with butter on his plate, while he continued. "All they do is complain and threaten not to work when they're not working hard anyway. Just wait until I explain it to the National Labor Relations Board. They *will* get an earful from me."

Over time, Dad had worked his way up to a comfortable middle management position in Human Resources. I was no business major, but it sounded to me like the humans there were not much of a resource. Nor were they very resourceful if they had to rely on an appointed person to talk for them. I could not grasp how people who were seemingly part of a team weren't able to come out victorious. Why were they unable to somehow better themselves and each other? I mean, isn't that the precise definition of a team?

I often heard locals lament about the town we all lived in. Word on the street was there were not many opportunities available, and that "the bosses" just thought they were better than everyone else. My young mind reasoned that since my dad held a management position, that must have meant it was his fault people were miserable—and also, mine.

How could I have friends if they perceived I couldn't relate to them because I thought I was better?

I imagined their thoughts toward me. *How dare you think you're better than us? You're not.*

Being judged for something you unquestionably know is not who you are or what you believe, but others are categorically convinced of, is hard to combat. It's kind of like arguing a false negative. To elaborate further, this is called an, "argument from ignorance[1]" (not my terminology, although, who am I to argue?).

An argument from ignorance is also known as an appeal to ignorance, wherein ignorance represents a lack of contrary evidence. It is an illusion in logic. It asserts that a premise is true because it has not yet been proven false, or a premise is false because it has not yet been proven true.

Basically, it's a big fat lie of crazy head-stuff that says, whatever we think about you is right, and it may cause you to make dumb decisions the rest of your life, while you try to prove us wrong. This is

---

1 https://www.logicallyfallacious.com/tools/lp/Bo/LogicalFallacies/56/Argument-from-Ignorance

a false dichotomy, excluding the possibility that there is insufficient evidence (i.e. accurate, non-judgmental knowledge) to begin with.

If Facebook was a thing back in my teens, my short bio blurb would have read: *Not thinking I'm better than you since Atari 2600. Unless you compete against, underestimate, or otherwise judge me. Then we will both be miserable.*

My hunch is that your bio blurb has also been written in response to other people's perceptions of you. A fight or flight response that, as humans, we are forced into, both unknowingly—when we are young, and unnecessarily—adapting as we get older.

Today, when you look at social influencers' content, what do you see? Just so you know, that questions is supposed to be loaded. I can tell you what *I* see, but it's going to be a different answer from yours. Why? The picture the influencer posted is the same. The words the influencer used are the same. The platform is the same. But where I may see a celebrity post and immediately think, *Are you serious with this right now?* you might see the exact same post and think, *Wow, she's awesome!*

What we must realize in this nonstop digital age is that no matter how transparent a person is, famous or not, we don't know them. We only know what we can see on the surface.

For instance, if you first started following someone you admire because of a picture she posted looking extra stylish or in shape, you might think of her as on-trend and healthy. If, however, you started following her after she became a mom who was dealing with her daughter's dad's swiveling head and constant cheating, then you might think of her as a mother and a strong, empowered, independent woman who's nobody's fool.

Whatever you perceive about a human being you don't truly know, has nothing to do with the legitimacy or authenticity of the person. Nor does it have anything to do with their bio blurb. I mean, aside from checking for proper wording and spelling errors, isn't the second editing check often, "Can I really say I did that?"

Rather, what is perceived about a person we don't truly know has everything to do with the box you've put them in—otherwise known as your assumptions. Let's be honest, being put in a box with a lid on it is suffocating. What are we, Christmas decorations? Gimme a break. No one wants to be confined to a reality that belongs to someone else.

If we're not careful, perception can become reality. It can also make us lazy. Perception can cause us to stop doing the hard work to find out if what we believe is indeed fact.

We make judgments when we first meet people. But some of us also have questions about the other person. *Are they nice? Are they cruel? Are they someone I can trust? Are they someone who will hurt me? What are they thinking about me?*

> **PERCEPTION CAN CAUSE US TO STOP DOING THE HARD WORK TO FIND OUT IF WHAT WE BELIEVE IS INDEED FACT.**

Secretly, especially if we are in need of a friend, we might mentally fight to like this new human being who has entered our life. We want what they offer us at face value to be true. We root for them to be caring, authentic, compassionate, and awesome. We will give them the benefit of the doubt to make our hopes reality—until they reveal their true character, hitting one of our emotional triggers. If we have a history of being hurt, we can immediately begin to close ourselves off and smother any potential for this person to overcome the defenses we've raised.

We rarely offer allowances for someone else's bad day. Erased from our memory are the many times sharp, unkind words have slipped from our own mouths. You know the kind of words I'm talking about—the ones that leave us wishing we could rewind and take back the damage. And if that wasn't bad enough, we're too embarrassed, impatient, or prideful to confess or even apologize. We can't be bothered to ask deep questions to better understand what experiences may have led to that person's thought process. Maybe they too are reacting from past hurts. We fail to realize that in our own reflex to duck and cover, *we* may have assumed the role of judge—no jury needed.

We do exactly what we feared would be done to us. Because some of us live at high alert, we must exercise extreme caution, knowing our defensive reaction could leave behind others who are wounded, shredded to bits by just our tongues. Then, as if a knife is plunged in the heart, we cut them out of our lives forever. Does this feel a little personal? It is. I've been using this defense since childhood.

Circa 1981, in an age when telephones were still connected to walls, it was easy to line up a play date. Danielle and Kim were both older than me—Danielle by three years and Kim, her younger sister, by two. I had mathematical difficulty figuring it out exactly, as they were both in the same grade.

They also had one older brother, Eric, who was in high school. His evenings were spent frequenting local bars. I think this had something to do with his attempts at avoiding their parents' arguing. I have a penchant for nicknames, and I used to call their dad "King Kong," because he seemed huge and hairy and scary to me. Even in my limited relational understanding at the time, I had a hunch the three siblings called him something else.

Throughout summers during our elementary school years, we slurped popsicles during the day and caught fireflies destined for Mason Jars at night. One searing and humid evening, Danielle, Kim and I were playing our standard devised game of "van tag," whereby we stood on either side of their dad's bright yellow-orange van (think kidnapper model) and tossed a beach ball over top. The idea was to blindly throw and catch the ball until someone missed, and it hit the ground. The person who dropped the ball sprinted to pick it up, ran around the van, and tried to tag one of the other two who had already jetted off in fits of laughter. As usual, my parents sat on the stoop of our two-stepped front porch, talking and cheering us on.

"Good job, Bether!" they yelled, as I scooted quickly around and around the van, dodging the ball for what seemed like an eternity. Playing with friends as a carefree little girl, no worries, sweaty forehead, matted hair, and seeing my parents sitting knee-to-knee, meant life was good. My favorite oak tree, stationed in our front yard, framed my happiness perfectly. Until my joy melted like a broken popsicle piece dropped on a sweltering sidewalk.

"Stop!" Danielle cried out. "This isn't fun. Stop going so fast. Stop making us look bad."

What? What did she mean, make them look bad? I thought I was playing by the rules—how is the game supposed to be played? Wait—what? What's happening, what changed?

I never had a chance to ask these questions out loud. The next thing I knew, Danielle and Kim grabbed their ball, stormed into their house, slammed the door and left me in the street staring back at my parents. With one final, "We hate you," spewed by Kim through an open front window, I was devastated.

Lickety-split, my friends labeled me. Enemy. As I type these words, my stomach still knots when I think about it.

Assumptions made about us by people in our close inner circle—friends, neighbors, family—are hard to shake. From birth to death, humans want and need a sense of belonging. This is fact. Loneliness is a bigger problem than simply having an emotional experience. When isolation or unbelonging occurs, subsequent living is grossly affected. We learn to suppress ourselves.

Feeling broken, I needed to understand what had just happened. "Mom, what did I do wrong?" Dirty tears streaked the back of my hand after I brushed it over my cheeks.

"Nothing, sweetie," she said.

"Well, I must have done *something*! They hate me."

Tears welled at the corners of my mother's eyes. Sadness covered her face like a dark cloud smothering the sun. My dad sat stone-cold, like a statue whose cool, porcelain exterior turned from white to bright red.

> **WHEN ISOLATION OR UNBELONGING OCCURS, SUBSEQUENT LIVING IS GROSSLY AFFECTED.**

My little sister watched us all—looking confused. That made two of us.

Mom exhaled deeply. "You didn't do a thing. You were playing and they were frustrated because they couldn't catch the ball as often as you, that's all," she said.

Wondering if I did something wrong, I interrupted. "Should I have let them win?

"That is a question you will wrestle with the rest of your life," she said.

To an eight-year-old me, it all seemed ridiculous. I didn't want to wrestle with anything other than the covers on my bed when I got cold at night. Why did my friends now suddenly hate me? And why, for the love of all things unknown to me, did I feel responsible for it all? That feeling would follow me like an unwanted shadow.

Words mean nothing against the backdrop of actions.

Mom bit her lip. "I think maybe Danielle and Kim felt badly about themselves because you usually win when you all play the game. Also, we were outside watching you and cheering, but their parents weren't."

> **WORDS MEAN NOTHING AGAINST THE BACKDROP OF ACTIONS.**

It was sort of making more sense to me, but I became defensive. "If they want to win so badly, shouldn't they try harder? It's either that, or I try less hard, right? I guess I'm the one who is supposed to fix this even though you just told me I didn't do anything wrong. I am so confused, Mom."

My sister rolled her eyes.

"Wait," I looked up through my sniffly tears. "What did you say about Danielle and Kim's parents?" It suddenly hit me, there might be more to Danielle and Kim's meanness, than I first thought.

"Their parents aren't around much, and yours are," Mom said.

Though I was only eight, I launched into a diatribe fit for a teenager. I knew right was right and wrong was unfair. "How is that my fault? Where are they anyway? They could be home if they wanted to, right?"

Done with the explanations, my mom said slowly, "I am going to tell you one last time and you're just going to have to believe me. It's not your fault. You were just being you."

An unhappy realization struck me. Me being me caused people to leave. That's the message I received. Words mean nothing against the backdrop of actions.

If me being myself equals abandonment, then who should I become?

This single question flooded my young brain then, but I can tell you, that was the beginning of me trying on innumerable watered-down versions of my real self.

REMORSELESS REMINDERS

- Human instinct drives us to label people—especially if they do something we don't like.

- You cannot force other people to stop labeling, but you can work on catching and stopping yourself.

- Everyone has stories they are not aware of that impact their reactions and behaviors.

- Misinterpretations, jealousies, and emotional triggers often lead to negative judgments and narrow views.

- Giving ourselves permission to consider our own pasts and learn about the pasts of others frees us to live empathetically.

CHAPTER 4

ASININE ASSUMPTIONS

Detecting O.P.O. a/k/a other people's opinions, takes adroitness. It requires a certain level of dexterity, along with a whole lot of careful consideration, before landing on a final verdict. And by verdict, I mean trying to answer the often unanswerable question that circles in our heads when we meet someone. *What are they assuming about me?*

It's a rather uncomfortable proposition, isn't it? Within the first seven seconds of meeting, people will have a solid impression of *who you are*—in actuality, a tenth of a second is all it takes to start determining traits like trustworthiness[2].

This is crazy to me. Absolutely unbelievable. How in the world can people begin to make character assumptions about us—even as important as whether or not we can be trusted—in less time than it takes to get a bowl of cereal in the morning? It's borderline implausible.

And yet, we assume things about others every day. It's simple human nature. We are created with certain intuitions designed to keep us safe, like knowing the dark alley we just stumbled into holds danger, or a restaurant that isn't actually serving food signals trouble. We instinctually know where danger lurks. However, the waters be-

---

2 https://time.com/5374799/best-first-impression-experts/

come a little more muddied when we bring our inherent compasses of assumptions into everyday realms with other human beings.

66 WE INSTINCTUALLY KNOW WHERE DANGER LURKS.

Regardless of venue, when you meet people, adult protocol dictates asking socially obligatory questions. "How are you? What do you do for a living? Where are you from? What brings you here?" etc. I do not truly love or enjoy these platitudes. I find them meaningless and disingenuous. It tends to feel like an inquisition, or an invasion of sorts.

During one particularly difficult time in my life, a female attorney I'd met through our running club, invited me to join her and a group of her colleagues for dinner. I think she felt sorry for me after I'd confided some of my woes as a single, divorced mom. Never one to turn down an event where there are new people to meet, I gladly accepted, readying myself in less than five minutes. This is how I found myself sitting in a swanky restaurant, surrounded by lawyers.

The day had been chaotic. I was trying to navigate singledom for the first time in over twenty years while raising a teenaged daughter. Neither is a walk in any kind of seasonal park. Thus, I wore what I wore.

If underdressed can ever be an understatement, please let the record show it here. In the throes and aftermath of divorce, when putting on a pair of sweats seemed monumental, I was pretty proud of myself when I managed to hoist a pair of jeans onto my still shaky legs. I wasn't entirely through the grieving process over my lost marriage.

I immediately felt as if the entire table was already cross-examining me when I walked into the restaurant. The room had no vestibule to offer protection from the peering eyes of its already seated diners. The male attorneys were decked out in suits, ties, and suspenders while my friend and the other lone female also wore business suits. Glancing down, I was thankful I had at least remembered a belt, to glitz up my Nike tee-shirt.

I took a deep breath, straightened my shoulders, and walked over to their table and introduced myself. "Hi. I'm Beth," I said, while offering a half-cheerful and mostly heartfelt smile.

Three of the eight of them said hello, including the two females in the group.

As I took an offered seat, I felt like a parrot among ravens, or like an adult sitting at the kids table during the holidays. Along with fewer pots and pans, divorce also leaves you with an immediate stigma and sense of unbelonging. No matter how out of sorts you feel, mercilessly, everyone still expects you to be ready with proper answers in social settings.

The question arrived before the waiter did. "What do you do for a living? Beth, is it?" The man's voice was smooth, with a drip of pretention. He wore big monogrammed cufflinks, a large insignia ring, and a diamond encrusted Rolex. When he spoke, all eyes at the table turned to him—there was no doubting who was in charge.

All side conversations stopped, as everyone waited for me to speak. I felt like an armed forces sniper must, counting back from five, finger on the trigger, slowing down each intentional breath before the moment of truth.

"I'm a proctologist," I said. I tried to keep my face straight, as I imagined one of my Facebook bios. The thought came to my rescue. Read: *Humor. Getting me through life and all its uncomfortableness for as long as I can remember.*

From the look on their collective faces, the attorneys must have assumed I'd tell them I was a barmaid. Which by the way, I used to be one, and I loved the job.

After letting them sweat it out a few more seconds, I smiled and clarified, "I'm in sales."

I got a couple of half-smiles for my truth, but only momentarily. Conversations moved on, and though they included me politely, the distinctions between the other people at the table and me were evident. I wasn't one of them.

It seemed clear they were thinking they were "better than" based on some irrelevant societal labels used—the have and have nots. What they didn't know about this have not though, is that I made it out of the house that day with belt intact. I was making progress and doing better than the day before.

I didn't yet know that transformation can occur even when we are sandwiched between scrutiny or scratching through situations wrought with despair. When we are in the middle of discomfort, it's hard to see transition taking place. I don't know if time heals all wounds, but it does bring about change. And I believe God used the deep grief of divorce to reframe the way I identified myself. He stripped away many of my asinine assumptions.

> **WHEN WE ARE IN THE MIDDLE OF DISCOMFORT, IT'S HARD TO SEE TRANSITION TAKING PLACE.**

I'm not a pessimistic person. I am the girl with the big smile, playful quips, and endless curiosity—excited to draw other people into my inherent optimism.

When I was a kid, I'd wait for the mailman at the end of the driveway every day, waving excitedly as he approached. Whether rain, sleet, snow, or hail, I waited for that mail-toting guy. It didn't matter if he handed me a stack of bills or a Publisher's Clearing House check—that kind of stuff has never been the point for me—people have. I was simply happy to see him.

That's how I think God intended it. It's never been about *what* people have—it's always been about *who people are.*

When marginalized or rejected, it's always felt contrary to who I really am. Part of me wants to shrivel up in a ball and be left alone forever, while the other part of me wants to scream like I've just come from my alma mater's national championship game and have no voice left. I want someone—anyone—to hear me. But most often, I can't even hear myself.

> **IT'S NEVER BEEN ABOUT *WHAT* PEOPLE HAVE— IT'S ALWAYS BEEN ABOUT *WHO PEOPLE ARE.***

During my divorce, I went from an optimistic, loving, energetic person to someone who could barely get out of bed. My can-do attitude was suddenly replaced with a dire, doomsday outlook. I felt unlovable. I could barely gather enough energy to make scrambled eggs for my daughter or wash my own hair. It was daunting on so many levels, but at the peak, it was the most debilitating because I couldn't even count on myself. The girl who could get through anything was gone.

Seated at a table surrounded by attorneys, I weighed how much work I'd done on myself in contrast to how I felt in that moment. Adjusting my bling-bling belt, I stopped calling the people around me names in my head, and instead silently talked to God, which was weird, because I'd never had an unscripted conversation with him in a crowd of people before. Some would say hearing God respond was debatable, and Lord knows there were enough debate club champions sitting at that table, but I was clear on what I sensed.

God reminded me of all I had been through, how far I had come, and how much deep and painful work it took for me to peel back the layers to reveal the truth in my soul. Regardless of the assumptions made by the people at that table, I managed to get through the remainder of the dinner. A few hours later, I walked into my house with my head held high. I knew that whatever tomorrow brought, I was one step closer to being wholly able to deal with it. Only I wasn't finished with the work yet.

During this season, crawling into my bed at the end of every day was one giant contradiction. On one hand, I was beyond bone-tired. The physical demands of taking care of a house on my own coupled with working full-time as a single parent was exhausting, so a bed that offered a place to rest and recuperate appealed to me. But on the other hand, it was just plain lonely. The only way I combatted the solitary chill was by filling my bed with books—including and especially, the Bible. So, when I returned home from my cross-examination-of-the-underachiever-on-the-witness-stand dinner, I knew exactly what I wanted to read to prevent my heart from turning calloused again.

I am literally all over the place when I open a Bible. Sure, I've read it front to back, but honestly? Some of those names in the Old Testament are whack, and as a perfectionist grammarian wannabe, it trips me up. I mean who names their kid Nahum anymore?

On this night, Luke 24 called my name. I hope after getting to know me, you were fairly certain I wasn't going to say, Proverbs 31. Just in case you are unfamiliar with those passages—Luke 24 is about women going to anoint Jesus' dead body but finding an empty tomb when they arrived. Proverbs 31 is about how to be a good woman or ideal wife. Both chapters have baffled me.

> **FOR ME, THE BIBLE BECAME A GREAT BEDMATE.**

Here's the deal. After not reading God's Word (at least in the form of an actual Bible) for the first thirty years of my life, discovering its comfort was better than sneaking downstairs on Christmas morning and having your awe-struck eyes land on a puppy wearing a red velvet bow. I can't stop hanging out with the Bible, mostly because it's like a gift that gets better each time you open it. I always discover something new, something I hadn't noticed or understood previously. Scripture is living and breathing and active, and we are all—if we choose to be—its proud owner.

For me, the Bible became a great bedmate.

I also want to say I appreciate Proverbs 31, just not in the stereotypical way. Thus, I blew by Proverbs en route to Luke in the New Testament that night. I could think of no more appropriate way to end such a farcical evening than to read a biblical book written by a doctor after spending an evening with lawyers. I also liked the fact that in Luke, Jesus appeared to three women who, in turn, told the men of their day what was up.

While other people will always have opinions of us, and, conversely, we of them, having the deftness to bob and weave when you feel under attack is crucial. In my long list of received and perceived assumptions, the most asinine to date has been that I am "not a very good Christian."

I'm not sure that anyone in the history of forever is ever going to agree on what a good Christian looks like. There was a time when

I thought I didn't measure up. According to some standards, I'm still not a good one.

I am convinced part of our spiritual growth includes analyzing if we are "good Christians" occasionally, sort of like doing a gut-soul-reality check. It's okay to wonder. It's okay to answer honestly. And it is certainly okay to disagree with someone who is not God. He is the One with truth answers, and he's the One who shows up when he knows you're good and ready.

We aren't being judged for our punctuality with God. There are no time slots or reservations we must make. Unlike the group of attorneys whose views of people are based on measurements of what they have or do, God sees us differently. We don't have to worry about what other people think—no matter the venue.

Besides, going out to eat with bad company is underwhelming. I'd much rather stay in with a good book.

REMORSELESS REMINDERS

- Ascertaining other people's opinions cannot be done in an offhanded manner.

- Making assumptions about others is human nature, but it's rarely accurate.

- When we are in the middle of a tough situation or season of life, it's hard to notice the transformation that's slowly occurring—but it is.

- Societal labels, i.e. classism, is obnoxious. Like most descriptors, viewing someone by what they do or don't have does not accurately define someone's character, and certainly not their real worth.

- The only way out of a deeply difficult situation is to go through it. Keep going!

CHAPTER 5

NARRATIVE LOOPS

Understanding others is like an Act of Congress. It's no small feat, and nothing short of miraculous if we're being honest.

People are complex, inconsistent, and will routinely let you down time and time again. But does that mean *everyone* is a no-good terrible loser? Man, if that's the case, then perhaps I shouldn't have said yes to marriage a third time. After all, my resume was already in danger of looking like Liz Taylor's.

I learned early when playing van tag with my neighbors, acceptance can feel fickle. One minute, Danielle and Kim liked me, and the next, I didn't have any friends. The same thing happened when I got older. One minute I was married, the next I wasn't. One minute I was valued and respected in church, the next I was snubbed. My list of shuns run long.

I've often wondered why people rejected me. Did they see me as an enemy? And if so, what in me caused them to think that way? Was there something silently signaling some serious deficiency in me? When people played nice in the beginning, only to turn on me as the relationship deepened, did it mean I was unlovable? Those seemed like reasonable questions, albeit ones for which answers weren't readily available.

I was conditioned to disbelieve the words people conveyed. I'm not proud of that, nor did I ever make a conscious decision to become cynical—I don't want to be. We've all been burned by someone who said one thing and did another, but not all of us fan those embers into a torch we use to hunt down and light up every lie. Illuminator might be my middle name.

The bottom line is I've carried distrust with me most of my life, which perpetuated both my doer tendencies and the crashing of many romantic relationships. I still struggle with receiving compliments. I would much prefer feelings be shown rather than said, primarily through a mutual understanding of not blabbering on with the drippy sweet nothings. You can show me all day long though, by putting your dishes in the dishwasher.

That's what matters to me. *Showing* love. What matters to you? What really speaks love to your heart? Not what the world tells you should be done—but what *really* makes you feel valued? Do you know?

There is an ongoing slippery-slope we must traverse in order to live as our real selves in the present. It requires us to look back with a high degree of introspective pragmatism, removing any hint of emotion in order to discern how our past experiences and presuppositions are informing our state of being today. Detaching from past emotional hurts isn't easy, but it is necessary in order for us to see through an unbiased lens, revealing the source of our limiting ways.

Life has taught me how people can both perceive and receive me—and how my narrative loops determine the way I perceive and receive others.

I'm sure there are people in your life as there are in mine, who are absolutely unaware. Not only are they oblivious to the idea of retrospect or learning from mistakes under the old adage of, "history often repeats itself," they are also incapable of growth.

At our most basic cellular levels we all want to know that we matter, vis-à-vis are understood. How many times has your teenager screamed, "You don't understand me!" in the middle of a heated argument whereby you again wonder if the mothership will be landing soon to retrieve them?

> **LIFE HAS TAUGHT ME HOW PEOPLE CAN BOTH PERCEIVE AND RECEIVE ME—AND HOW MY NARRATIVE LOOPS DETERMINE THE WAY I PERCEIVE AND RECEIVE OTHERS.**

Understanding and being understood are paramount to relationship. If you do not understand the other or feel understood, then *other* eventually equals *alone*. And I'm not talking about being alone with an *Us*® magazine and a Chipotle® bowl at the counter, sitting on a window stool.

I'm talking about people who haven't discerned the necessity of changing, growing, or learning from past mistakes. They stay stuck in some previous version of themselves—continually playing an old narrative on loop. You may know the type.

"When I played football in high school, I was unstoppable. Those skinny quarterback losers didn't even see me comin! I pummeled them so hard they didn't know what hit 'em."

Okay, dude—you're fifty. That was a million years ago, why are we still talking about this?

Because they're stuck, that's why.

"I was never happier than when I called my boys to the table for supper. We used to laugh so much, and my Tommy couldn't get enough of my cooking."

Really? My husband has a different recollection. And he's an adult now. His name his Tom.

Some mothers have a particular struggle with releasing their children into a world that doesn't revolve around them.

I used to feel guilty for having no tolerance for those types of narrative loops. Not anymore.

When you're trying to transform and grow, it's hard to be around people who insist on staying stuck in a memory time warp. Before I found freedom, I had to do the hard work of my own introspective pragmatism. Once I gave myself permission to keep moving forward, I reminded myself that I didn't have to get sucked into someone else's vortex.

"You should have seen me when I ran track in seventh-grade!" a man in his late forties mentioned to me in passing one day.

No, I shouldn't have, I thought.

> **❝ ONCE I GAVE MYSELF PERMISSION TO KEEP MOVING FORWARD, I REMINDED MYSELF THAT I DIDN'T HAVE TO GET SUCKED INTO SOMEONE ELSE'S VORTEX.**

With newfound permission to only look forward, I found my footing. I felt lighter, like I could stand straight again. I stopped trying to atone for being me. I stopped trying to alter myself at my core, just so others would be more comfortable. I stopped pretending so others would hate me a little less.

I began to feel more proficient at life, experiencing a whole new freedom I never knew existed. Did this happen overnight? That may be the funniest question of all time.

Not even close. In fact, it took me many years and many more

NARRATIVE LOOPS

(like a zillion) hard life lessons and soul-crushing failures to even realize revolution was happening inside me. Through my incessant questions and competitiveness, I eventually unearthed my narrative patterns. I discovered they started early.

When I was twelve, I passed the summer by visiting the local library, usually from open to close. Each morning, I greeted the librarian and chatted with her while she unlocked the front door. My early arrival ensured I'd be first in and fill my basket with all the good picks: *A Tale of Two Cities, The Catcher in the Rye, To Kill a Mockingbird, I Know Why the Caged Bird Sings, The Bell Jar.*

The head librarian's name was Mrs. Lamb. I always found that a ludicrous name, kind of like reverse personification since only males are referred to as lambs. But no one asked me, nor did I ask her if there was a Mr. Lamb who caused that faux pas. She liked me—until she didn't. I encountered her newfound disdain for me one day when I asked her about available reading selections, or more specifically, lack thereof.

"Mrs. Lamb, where can I find *The Fall of the House of Usher*?" I asked her politely.

"The what?" she responded.

I repeated the title, slower this time, "*The Fall of the House of Usher,* by Edgar Allan Poe."

"Oh. We don't have him in our library. Too vulgar."

"Who decided that?" I asked her, well-intended but I'm sure, in hindsight, not coming across as such. "I mean, isn't vulgarity a form of expression, kind of like art?"

Silence.

I waited. I had all day. Summer and all.

"I'm not sure who decided, but we do not have *The Fall of the House of Usher* in our library, Beth."

"Well, okay, how about *The Tell-tale Heart?*"

I think she thought that was rhetorical based upon her painful facial contortions.

I finally resigned myself to reading *The Very Hungry Caterpillar* to the incoming toddlers and *I Know Why the Caged Bird Sings* to myself. I was grateful that Maya Angelou wasn't also banned for being too vulgar.

Going to the local pool also became drudgery that summer. Once you passed the deep-end lap test, there wasn't much else to achieve. For a while, I supplemented swimming on the other side of the roped buoys by practicing my diving skills. I had not intended to do this until I read a sign that changed my mind. It read, DIVING COMPETITION NEXT WEEK. TOP THREE PLACES RECEIVE A PRIZE.

How hard can it be? I thought.

Apparently, a smidge more difficult than I imagined. My welted and stinging stomach reminded me of this for the next six days. Each morning at 10:00 a.m., when the pool opened, I was the first one through the gross and slimy entrance. After showing the gum-cracking employee our family pool pass ticket, I hustled through, dropped my towel and hit the high dive. In and out of the water I went, landing a little less like an Orca whale each time. It wasn't pretty, but I persevered in spite of my form.

"All those ages 12-18 who would like to enter the diving competition, please head to the platform now," a voice on the loudspeaker announced.

I knew that voice. It was Joe Breckson. Joe was a senior and the high school quarterback. He rolled around town in his dad's blue Camaro with Van Halen blasting through the speakers and a skinny glass Pepsi bottle quenching his thirst at every red light. This meant circling, since we only had a couple of streetlights in town.

I always thought it a stumper as to how he could sing every word, never miss a beat, still manage to drive with only one hand, and hold his Pepsi with his arm draped over some girl's shoulder. From what I observed, Joe liked the type of female who laughed at his dumb jokes and basically had no skills other than availability.

But this was competition day. I started walking toward the platform, wondering to myself, *Is Joe Breckson going to be the sole judge of this thing?* Sure, he was a lifeguard, but by definition, I wasn't too convinced that he could guard any lives, let alone evaluate anything other than his own reflection.

Great, I thought. All this work for nothing.

Joe took his seat in his captain's lifeguard chair which was directly in the center of the round pool. He sat in the center of the water, which in the summer, was the hub of the village. Positioned with a clear view of the pool, the main traffic light provided an instant audience each time it turned red.

I stood on the platform with two other girls. Somehow that fact increased the flow of my competitive juices even more. I was determined to win. There was no way I was walking away with a third-place trophy or whatever dumb-darn thing the pool could afford to give away. Third-place in this instance, meant loser.

This is it. People in town can watch me get my prize, I thought while I waited for the start signal.

I went first. Confidently, I climbed the two slippery metal steps up to the board and took my position. With a glance over my left shoulder at Joe seated upon his throne, I avoided eye contact and began my methodical three step approach. I had practiced my precise routine preceding the jump no less than two hundred times over the course of six days.

One ... two ... three ... spring ... jump high ... and ... GO!

Up through the air I went, hinging my hips at exactly the right time as my legs came together in unison. I could feel my ankles touch and my heart pounding. My hands broke the entry into the water. *This is exactly what Greg Louganis must feel like*, I thought. The exhilaration was almost too much to take.

My head popped up, just as I heard two or three faint hand claps.

Seriously? That's it? Whatever.

It was my best dive of the week. Only it wasn't enough.

The next day, I saw the first-place winner in the front seat of Joe Breckson's Camaro. Apparently, she was his prize after he awarded her the trophy.

Unsure of whose head I wanted to tear off more, his or hers, somewhere deep within me, I realized I was the one who had been fractured and torn. Still, I didn't yet have the right words or enough worldly experiences to explain why.

I turned away, my narrative loop once again reinforcing that people saw me as less-than. I now felt that not only were messages in books subjective, but achievement was equally biased. If that's how people were going to judge me, if baselines were not clear, I would have to protect myself from future disappointment. I got really good at it.

Twenty-five years after I practiced my diving skills, I debated whether or not I should attend a neighborhood holiday party. We don't always get adequate warning when a person, place, or similar situation will come back around. What I wasn't properly prepared for was the circle of life's beautiful mess.

Just a few months prior, my marriage ended. I had married a second time in the midst of utter life chaos, and after twelve years, had failed spectacularly at marriage *again*. It seemed surreal. I couldn't process it, and the entire experience instantly made me a million percent distrustful. Thus, I decided right then and there that I was never *ever* getting married again. In fact, I thought joining a convent sounded nice. A vow of celibacy and no men? Sign me up, sister.

> **WHAT I WASN'T PROPERLY PREPARED FOR WAS THE CIRCLE OF LIFE'S BEAUTIFUL MESS.**

Since I was certain I wouldn't pass the requisite convent entrance exam, I instead buried myself in work and school. I had started a master's program for my first theology degree three years prior, but because of the stress and tension from a crumbling marriage, I stopped. My impending single status seemed to signal a good time to start again. My evenings were wide open.

I both appreciated and loathed the ironic timing of my new *Marriage and Family Counseling* class, where we were taught that the demise of a marital relationship is horrific. Thanks for that light-bulb moment—*Am I paying for this class?* But when the lesson turned to the impact on an entire family, including and especially the kids, my pain level was off the charts. Thinking about the effect our divorce had on our respective children—who did absolutely nothing to cause the demise of our marriage—was absolutely the hardest part for me to reconcile and get through. I often cried over the memories we'd made together, including family dinners, sporting events, and celebrating milestones and holidays.

So, suffice it to say, deciding to attend a neighborhood party that had become tradition, conjured up apprehension. The thought of walking into that party with people who, at one point in my life, knew me as a married woman with a family, did not hold appeal. While I didn't send anyone a folded note asking them to circle YES or NO in response to, "Will this be awkward if I attend by myself?" I already thought I knew the answer.

Familiar narrative loops played in my head. *You know the looks you'll get as soon as you walk in. Everyone will be talking about you. They'll want to know what happened. You're the potential enemy now. Even the ones who pretend to like you will whisper when you leave. Why would you put yourself through that? Just stay home.*

But I knew if I was going to help everyone heal and get through that terrible time, I needed to move beyond my fears and insecurities. The situation wasn't all about me. Divorce is far-reaching with its implications. I needed to set an example of maturity and unselfishness. It was also imperative for my own soul—my own transformative growth—that I did not allow my emotions to limit an opportunity to change the narrative playing in my head.

I made it through that year's holiday party. And so, did everyone else.

I did it by telling myself that I truly can't know what other people are thinking about me—if they are at all. Even if people are casting judgments and assumptions on me, they're likely coming from a place of their own hurts. Maybe no one has told them how important they are, so they struggle to find their worth by focusing on other people's weaknesses. Maybe they are in the midst of something similar and don't want to think about their own pain in that moment. Maybe they are fighting their way back to normalcy. Or, maybe they just don't like cheese plates and veggie trays. Again—

you just can't know for sure, but you can always choose to do the right thing.

REMORSELESS REMINDERS

- People are complex, inconsistent, and will let you down—don't let it jade you.

- People are also kind and good—welcome their help when you need it.

- Narrative loops reinforce with repetition—you can change your internal messages.

- Familiar narratives can become hard to recognize, catching them takes intentional practice.

- Expect transformation to take time and celebrate small successes along the way.

CHAPTER 6

WATERED-DOWN VERSION

Medal-less after the dive competition, but still principled, I got a job, since I was now more bored than ever.

I convinced myself that even though I had been deprived of a prize, there were bigger injustices at play. Not fully understanding my own emotions, my thought was simply that the proud owner of the diving trophy should use it to club Joe what's-his-face over the head. She also might take some diving lessons in her spare time, so in the future she could win on merit, not flirtations. But I soon tired of replaying the senselessness and decided to move past questions I couldn't answer, and I went to work instead.

My first official place of employment was at a nearby golf course. Every summer, beginning when my sister and I were seven and ten respectively, our family frequently spent time together playing rounds of golf. Into my teens, we tried various courses in the Midwest.

Dad and Mom only took us on weekdays, when games were cheaper, and the greens were less populated with golfers. My parents were not serious players, but they were good enough to swear when balls were lost or hit straight into the water on par threes. Those outings still constitute some of my favorite memories. I loved riding around in a golf cart, enjoying the summer night's heat, and listening to peaceful sounds of nature. This was how we spent quality family time together and figured out how to win rounds. I got schooled more than once and in more than one way.

"Dad, can I hit one?" I said. "I think I can get it over that pond."

He laughed. He had just lost three balls to one course's murky abyss, and his driver, while not in the water, wasn't locatable from where we stood. Our view only revealed a grove of giant pine trees and the grassy green. Its flag waved in the wind, which I found to be a taunt if not an invitation.

"Sure, go ahead," Dad said, a smirk on his face cementing his bet on the outcome.

I grabbed what I hoped was the right club from the back of my mom's cart and marched up to the tee box.

"You need one of these, dummy," my sister, the illusory caddy pointed out. She threw a tee at me.

Once planted in the ground, ball on top, I proceeded to hit that Titleist as hard as I would later want to hit some of my employer's prominent members.

"Whew, we! What a shot!" my dad yelled. I loved making him proud, even more than I loved proving him wrong.

I was smiling. Another woman, whom I found out later actually lived in a cabin in the middle of the course, did not look pleased.

"Nice shot, girl," she said as we drove the golf cart over the bridge on the way to what I would learn is called a birdie shot.

I heard her complimentary words, but her face indicated displeasure. My formerly happy and carefree soul filled with an unsettling angst. I knew the variances in her words and body language meant conflict.

I've always had a proclivity for watching people—not in some weird, creepy way, but rather to see what they were trying to accomplish, and oftentimes, so I could figure out a way to help them succeed. To me, everyone should be afforded the same possibilities in life. I operated under the notion that people are equal. No one is better or more deserving than another. Not even Joe, the lifeguard.

Working in a clubhouse as a cashier, grill-line cook, and server seemed like a good first job fit, since being on a golf course elicited positive feelings for me. But it was also where my continuing education in expectations and injustices occurred. I wasn't forewarned that more unaligned words and actions would confuse and disappoint me.

> ## NO ONE IS BETTER OR MORE DESERVING THAN ANOTHER.

I was thirteen, fully enjoying the summer before high school began. None of my other friends had jobs yet, and in fact, they found it shocking that I was gainfully employed by choice. I found it baffling that they weren't. Other than evening softball games on the women's league team, what was there to do? One could only sleep so long.

During my first and only job interview, the manager of the clubhouse warned me about my potential future boss. "Shel is slightly gruff and smokes a lot," he said.

Since my parents and many others also smoked a lot back then, his admonishment didn't strike me as anything to be worried about. I was more intrigued by Shel's name. *Shel.* I'd never read or heard a name like that before, so I found it interesting. I figured it was either a nickname or a joke. But after my mom dropped me off on my first day of work and I met my new supervisor, I quickly deduced nothing was a joke about this woman.

After only a few minutes, I decided a better description of Shel was a battle-axe who slung skinny menthols out of her wrinkled mouth around the clock. My first interaction with her set the tone.

"You Beth?" Shel muttered through tightly clenched lips so as not to lose her smoke stick.

"Yes," I said, trying to sound appropriately intimidated, but really wondering why she was still employed.

"Git yourself behind the counter, put on that there apron, and come 'round with the coffee. The men will be gittin' here soon to eat."

The apron was stained, and the coffee was thick like tar. I wondered, *What kind of men would want to come here to eat?*

Turns out, the kind who had zero respect for any female.

"Git your pretty little buns over here and fill up my cup, sugar," one old, giant and unkempt man said. He wore an ill-fitting plaid golf ensemble and sat at a table of with a group of other disrespectful look-alikes.

For several seconds, I didn't move, taking the surreal scene in. Shel's glare finally motivated me to action, one I repeated throughout the morning. I talked myself through doing what Shel instructed, while simultaneously enduring verbal assaults from customers. Many inner debates ran through my mind, until I was accosted again by another sloppy old man.

"You're so beautiful." He laughed in a way that I knew wasn't funny, elbowing his buddies.

"Beth, they's a talkin to you. Go'n git!" Shel snapped from her roost behind the counter.

Like deja vu, I didn't move.

In retrospect, I know I stood my ground on the basis of principle. I instinctually knew no one should speak to another human being in that manner. And clearly . . . clearly on the basis of *excuse me, old man? You might believe I am just a dumb little girl but think again. And why are you eyeing me like I'm a slice of warm apple pie with a side of vanilla ice cream?*

"Beth! He's a talkin' to you!" Shel barked.

My head had no more room for thoughts at that point, except to mentally tell Shel she needed to get lost. And then to immediately feel guilty for thinking about her that way, as incomprehensible as it is to me now. As a woman, I realize Shel had probably endured the same kind of behavior I was being subjected to. In that moment though, I also believed I had no choice but to listen to my boss.

The younger me felt disillusioned. Weren't older women supposed to stick up for soon-to-be women? Is this what working will look like the rest of my life? Will I always have to endure men speaking to me disrespectfully in order to make money and someday support myself? Deep inside my soul, I felt such despair and powerlessness, knowing there was nothing I, a young teen, could do to right this blatant wrong.

Shel's burrowing stare propelled my legs to move. I stepped up to the table and poured the black sludge into coffee cups, under the leering eyes of the men. Forcing cheer into my tone, I asked, "Would any of you like some bacon? There's plenty here to go around."

Sardonic humor is something my parents handed down from parent to child. While I can't pinpoint where my response came from for sure, I do know that somewhere, buried deep within my psyche, resided a little girl dressed like Scrappy-Doo, the beloved nephew of Scooby-Doo. She shouted from my mind, "Put 'em up! I dare ya!" Even then, I was ready to fight at any given moment to defend principles, to uphold a person's worth, as well as my own—even when I had to hide it under the veil of sarcasm.

There's just one problem with my inherent defense mechanism.

I don't want to respond with a scathing tongue. I want to operate solely on the basis of *being* me—a little ornery, yet deeply loving. I want to have enough control over my life, my own being, so the external behaviors of others cannot dictate my days, my choices, and my responses. But since I was being treated like less than me, I felt I had no choice but to serve a little sarcasm with their coffee.

> **I WANT TO HAVE ENOUGH CONTROL OVER MY LIFE, MY OWN BEING, SO THE EXTERNAL BEHAVIORS OF OTHERS CANNOT DICTATE MY DAYS, MY CHOICES, AND MY RESPONSES.**

Standing in a bustling golf course restaurant, schlepping food, sweat pouring off my brow, I explicitly chose to live like a discounted, imposter version of myself. Trapped. Isn't that always one of the worst places to be?

I changed that day. On a random Saturday morning in my thirteenth year, I lost another layer of my trusting view of people and my ability to rightly assess my choices, by letting others push me around and accepting their watered-down version of myself. It was hard to drown out inappropriate noise, which left me feeling defeated in my fight against injustice.

Had I only known scripture back then, maybe I could have resorted to biblical humor to get me through. I could have shouted, "You might as well be a bunch of eunuchs!" in an effort to defend myself. Or, maybe I could have simply remembered I'm not the first woman who's felt used and disrespected at the whim of people in power—this kind of abuse goes back to ancient times.

Vashti is my kind of girl. I feel like maybe she and I would hang out if she was still alive today.

On the seventh day, when King Xerxes was in high spirits from wine, he commanded the seven eunuchs who served him . . . (seven names no one can pronounce, insert my sardonic humor). *. . . to bring before him Queen Vashti, wearing her royal crown in order to display her beauty to the people and nobles, for she was lovely to look at,"* (Esther 1:10-11 NIV).

Trust me when I say, at thirteen I did not feel lovely. I felt pubescent, uncertain, insecure, and scared. I wasn't in a position to pull a Queen Vashti move.

"But when the attendants delivered the king's command, Queen Vashti refused to come," (Esther 1:12).

Whether or not the Book of Esther is metaphorical or literal, having similar hutzpah to Vashti's response would have come in handy for me, my first day at work. It would have no doubt provided resolve for me to speak truth.

"How was your first day in the restaurant?" my mom asked excitedly, as I hopped in the car. I reeked of cooking grease and defeat.

"It was fine," I said, trying hard to sound Academy Award-worthy.

"Was Shel as interesting as you expected?"

"No, I wouldn't use interesting to describe her."

A side-effect of diminishing ourselves is watering down and hiding truths. It's a natural reaction, but the consequences are altogether different when cowering under completely innocuous circumstances, versus starting an unhealthy pattern that causes you to hide your true identity for years. We make choices in every situation. I made mine.

> **A SIDE-EFFECT OF DIMINISHING OURSELVES IS WATERING DOWN AND HIDING TRUTHS.**

Over time, I came to love my first job—and even Shel. The life-lessons I learned after I was given an opportunity to work while still a young teenager, were invaluable. I gained time-management, accountability, and people skills. As added bonuses, I also learned how to make a decent grilled hamburger and improved my golf score. My point is this, even in the best possible situations and circumstances, the onus is on us to make a decision. We must decide what we are worth in order to recognize the kind of treatment and behavior we will accept from others—and in turn—the kind we won't. How we decide will affect much of what happens to us in the future.

WATERED-DOWN VERSION

REMORSELESS REMINDERS

- Life situations can cause us to respond in ways that are in conflict with who we truly are. Fight against counterintuitive responses.

- When we reduce ourselves, watering-down truths causes side-effects.

- Generational injustices must always be confronted.

- People will treat you how you allow them to.

- Keep showing up—you never know when a perceived adversary will teach you skills.

CHAPTER 7

TWO SIDES TO EVERY COIN

Even when you think there should be someone else looking out for you, someone else who stands up for you against societal, age-old injustices and "boxed-in" expectations, at the end of the day, you're kinda on your own. Except and until, you know God.

As early as pre-kindergarten, I had a sense there was more to life than what I saw on the surface. And I don't mean in a way like, *Oh, I bet there's a house I've never seen before around the corner if I go down that street.* I mean more like, *There has GOT to be more in this world than this*—more than me, than right here, right now where I am sitting in Minerva, Ohio.

> " **I'VE COME TO BELIEVE THERE IS ABSOLUTELY SOMETHING GREATER THAN EACH OF US ORCHESTRATING THE BIGGER VISION OF LIFE ON PLANET EARTH.**

I realize those thoughts were perhaps outside the normal realm of thinking for a pint-sized girl not supposed to be old enough for deductive reasoning. I didn't know what I sensed with any sort of absoluteness, and I certainly couldn't explain it. I could only *feel* that it was true. The older I've gotten, however, the more I've seen confirmation supporting my premise. I've come to believe there is absolutely something greater than each of us orchestrating the bigger vision of life on planet earth.

In the era of disco music and American Bandstand, I had no idea how small, relatively-speaking, Minerva was compared to the rest of the world. When you're little, everything seems *gargantuan*. We lived in a nine-hundred square foot house, yet I somehow managed to find my own space inside. My friends and I played sports at a nearby park. We walked, but it seemed like it took twelve hours for us to reach the grassy playground. Clearly, my sense of spatial measurement was off. Hence, that presence I couldn't explain? The nameless, formless, nebulous, invisible "something greater out there?" Eventually, it just seemed too immense and distant to figure out.

So, I turned my focus onto another less profound subject.

Ah, relationships. I wish I'd understood the human condition before I started dating.

I'm Italian and Irish. Thus, two things were certain. I was going to grow up Catholic. And I was going to value tradition and sentimentality on an unwaveringly deep level.

I met my first Italian boy when I stood on the pitcher's mound at Rotary Park in Minerva. I was nine. He was eleven.

My dad coached me during my Rotary Club softball career until high school, when I became a player on the summer women's league. Dad led daily practices each season. He lobbed dependable pitches to us, and explained at length, the difference between fielding and batting to the team members whose parents had force-encouraged them to participate. We trained dutifully, always relieved to finally play for real scores.

Ten total fielders were in the game at any given time—six in the infield and four in the outfield. None of us were really developed enough to hit, so having a right and left center fielder seemed like defensive overkill. But it kept girls off the bench and minimized parental complaints. Dad loved baseball, rules, and teaching; thus, most everyone thought he made a great coach. He decided who played what position and batted in what order.

He put me fourth in the batting lineup and I pitched. In defense for his decision to place me there, I could swing the bat and throw strikes better than most of my teammates. Dad had to endure a few sideline parents who accused him of "only playing his kid where his kid wanted to play," but his piercing glare from behind the clipboard or my new base hit usually squelched their commentaries.

In one particular game, bottom of the ninth, with two down and one out to go, bases loaded and a full count, I stood on the pitching mound. Our team was one game away from an undefeated season and a guaranteed first seed in the upcoming tournament. I heard a voice from the sidelines yell out, "Hey! Here's a coloring book for you. Throw a strike and I'll throw in a free box of crayons."

To this day, I have no idea why the thought of a coloring book appealed to me. Even at age nine, I preferred to read words on a page conveying unlimited possibilities and potentials, rather than moving my hands back and forth between predefined lines. It wasn't the kind of prize that naturally motivated me, however, the dare did.

I looked over at the sidelines to see where the voice came from. I froze. A boy I'd never seen before lounged on a grassy hill with nothing but the first base line and a field of dirt between us. He wore the most beautiful grin I had seen in my nine years on the planet. His black hair shone under the afternoon sun and his big brown eyes sparkled against skin the color no box of Crayolas contained. I was awestruck.

And he was looking directly at *me*.

Time seemed to stop. The heat in my face told me its color had shaded to a red matching my uniform. My stomach churned in a way I had never felt before. Could a delay of game be called against a fourth-grade club team like the pro games on TV? I had no idea. I had no idea about anything in that moment. Everything and everyone seemed to melt away except that brown-eyed boy and me. I later found out his name was Jason.

Somewhere through my foggy brain, I began to hear my teammates yelling at me. When I picked up my dad's voice doing the same, I snapped out of it. But before I wound up my pitch, I met Jason's doe-like eleven-year-old eyes again. He repeated his Crayola dare—wanting an answer to the impending bet. I nodded.

I knew I'd throw a strike. What I didn't know was how the story and trajectory of my entire life was about to change.

For Jason's part, his first mistake was betting against me. His second was asking me to be his girlfriend.

Mine was saying yes.

In our community, girls who played sports could not tolerate being in the vicinity of girls who only *cheered* for boys who did. Please. Why would they:

a) not just lace up and play the game themselves when many of them were better than the high school boys they were rooting for?

b) fuel the stereotype?

These types of irreconcilable thoughts made me wonder why any girl would don an ugly and revealing pleated skirt, then jump and screech about a boy who acted like he was king of the court. In my mind, they should simply go be queen of the court.

Today, as a strong, independent, mature woman, I am a cheerleader for other females, no matter what they choose to do. It took me many years to understand that women should encourage each other. When we raise one, we lift all.

At age nine, I was too young, enamored, and yes, competitive, to know that every time you subtract a negative from your life, you make room for more positives. I definitely didn't understand the inverse was true. My season of terrible decision-making was about to commence.

Clearly one could not officially "date" at age nine, especially with a cautious father-coach. I only saw Jason once a week at church, which was fine by me. That was enough to look forward to.

> **EVERY TIME YOU SUBTRACT A NEGATIVE FROM YOUR LIFE, YOU MAKE ROOM FOR MORE POSITIVES.**

Our small house only had one tiny bathroom with a dwarf-sized tub. We did at least have a wall mounted sprayer that helped me get all the shampoo out of my thick hair before the hot water heater ran through all its reserve. In the basement, we had an eerie shower that could only be accessed from behind the ping-pong table after going through a saloon-style, green painted door. But I didn't mind it.

Once in a while, if I asked in advance, my dad let me shower down there. He kept the area meticulously clean, with organized towels folded in exactly the same proportions and no bent corners. Apparently, I "shed like a dog" and made a mess of Dad's pristine shower stall, so on Sunday mornings before church, I had to get ready upstairs. This meant I had to awaken three hours before Mass, since Mom and my sister, Sarah, also had to prep and primp. I needed enough time to create the appearance of a proper Catholic girl, and one Jason would want to stare at from across the aisle.

His family always sat on the left side of the church, four pews back, while our family always sat on the right side, either in the front or somewhere about half-way back. It was totally dependent on whether a prominent-in-the-area family attended. If that family of nine showed up, we sat more towards the back, allowing them to take up the entire front row.

Regardless of where we ended up in church, I only cared where one congregant sat. The other thirty or forty didn't matter as long as I could see his shiny black hair. Even his profile was perfect. At nine and in love, everything about him was perfect.

St. Gabriel's was the only Catholic church in the village. It was small and quaint and ancient. I learned all I needed to know about God and "the Catholics" from within the old, original brick building, just east of downtown's aptly named Main Street.

Missing Mass was out of the question. We did not miss for any reason. Every Sunday morning at 10 a.m. sharp, the organ began playing in anticipation of Father Mike's procession down the aisle—all of about six steps. He marched to the beat of four boring quarter notes and Mrs. O'Neal's smile, positioned from a cushioned bench seat, playing as if she was staged for her Grammy nomination. Everyone raised their hymnals high in the air, exactly beneath their chins no matter their height, and then collectively sang. At the finish, all simultaneously ceased.

Father Mike's voice boomed in the small sanctuary. "In the name of the Father and of the Son and of the Holy Spirit. Amen."

Finally. We could sit for a few minutes before we had to know when to kneel and stand and sit and shake. It was very on cue, dog-owner-like, I thought.

Regardless of denomination, you may be able to relate to this, if you have any childhood church background. What I'm sharing with you is my experience, and therefore, my perception of reality from the time. To my inquisitive and immature mind, it seemed like this: someone unknown to me pre-decided when I needed to sit and stand and kneel and say things I didn't understand, and mean things I didn't necessarily mean. It made the whole thing feel robotic and fake. Forced.

But even though I wrestled with what felt like a dictatorship mandate instead of a warm invitation, I was mostly concerned with the choreography over the homily. My priority was making sure I had the moves down so no one would judge me for kneeling, standing, sitting, or reciting wrong. I didn't want to add another punch to my certain bus ticket to Hell. I had no idea *why* I worried about this concern of mine.

- Was it just the way I was wired?

- Was it because I always wanted to win and be right and get whatever prize was being offered?

- Or was it simply because I was afraid of going to Hell for doing something wrong?

Yes. Yes, to all. But mostly, because I was deathly afraid of going to Hell. How about that for a hysterical oxymoron? Deathly afraid to die.

I was also deathly afraid to ask my parents or anyone else in church about who God really was. To do so would be to question the very One we were there to serve, and sing about, and worship. You know what happens to *those* people. Hell.

As my sweet Italian grandmother would say, I was so *avvitata*.

In that moment though, all I really was—was afraid. I was so painstakingly, gut-wrenchingly, soul-crushingly scared of God.

I craved answers. I wanted to know why God made me in such

a way that my brain constantly questioned why we were doing certain things in Mass. I wanted to know why my little rebellious-self wanted to laugh at Father Mike, instead of listen to him. I wanted to know why God created me in such a way that I thought mischievous thoughts for no reason and over which I had no control, but for which I would go to Hell for having the thoughts in the first place.

Wait—what?

Was it a set up? Was the system rigged? How do you get off this non-stop thought rollercoaster and win the prize? And, just to be sure—*is the prize not going to Hell?*

It was like I had a teeny-tiny band monkey inside my head, moving ever so calculatingly slowly. Back and forth, back and forth, between the left side of my brain and the right, as he beat his little heaven-hell drum.

Please tell me why I can't ask God about this directly? Why can I only talk through Mary, one of the saints, or a priest?

I knew enough to know I needed God's help. Directly. Not being allowed to ask The Creator for fear of being disrespectful and irreverent to *The Creator* was confusing.

I was brave enough to ask a catechism teacher about this deep-seated conundrum only once. The teacher made me feel two inches small. "How would it make God feel if you asked God why he made you like that? Wouldn't it make God feel angry that you are so ungrateful for being alive?"

Make God angry? What about me?

It took me years to unhear that teacher's answer. Having adults project confusing assumptions about God's character on me happened from my earliest memories. This is not uncommon. In fact, most of our bewilderment regarding 'religion' stems from attending church in our developmental years. We are malleable—so, understandably, we can't help but wonder if God is, too. Our young minds are trying to work out a potential disparity between *ourselves* and God, in whose image we are made. My swirling thoughts about God and me began early.

My first recollection of going to church at all was in Ashtabula, Ohio, where my parents were born and raised. It's also where they met and married. I lived the first four years of my life there, so my remembrance of being in one of my grandparent's Catholic churches for the first time in my life was prior to 1976.

> **OUR YOUNG MINDS ARE TRYING TO WORK OUT A POTENTIAL DISPARITY BETWEEN *OURSELVES* AND GOD, IN WHOSE IMAGE WE ARE MADE.**

While my parents were both from the same city in Ohio, they were also from different sides of the tracks—or in this case, different sides of the bridge. Ashtabula is on Lake Erie. My dad grew up in the harbor, while my mom grew up not in the harbor. She was from up-town, which is another way to say what everyone knew but pretended not to—people from the harbor area didn't have much money. People from up-town did.

The contrasts were rather stark.

There was a Carlisle's department store up-town. Amongst other luxuries, Carlisle's contained the very first elevator in Ashtabula. The harbor had a dime-store.

There were parks and convertibles up-town. The harbor had coal mines and bicycles.

Up-town was monochromatic. People in the harbor were blue collar, uneducated laborers who were called names I didn't understand for a long time, but somehow deduced through context that they meant something worse than just lazy. And in our family, being lazy was very bad.

The dualistic upbringing of my parents taught me there are always two sides to every story and spin. This especially includes theology and one's view on God. But I had no clue about that then.

All I knew was that if I went to my Italian grandmother's church in the harbor, she greeted everyone by their first name. When she introduced me, the other sweet, purse-clenching elderly ladies pinched my cheeks and called me sweetheart. And if I went to my Grandma Rit's up-town church, they didn't. I could not understand why, if people inside of different churches were worshiping the same God, they acted differently. Nor could I figure out, if all people are made in God's image, which images were right? Who should I act like? *Who am I? Who is God?*

REMORSELESS REMINDERS

- We can become easily enamored when introduced to new people and ideals. It can take many years to confirm whether initial feelings are in our best, long-term interest.

- Every person is created with a deep-seated curiosity about something greater than self.

- Carefully fostering mental acquisitiveness is necessary in order to quell fears.

- People's backgrounds, upbringings, and differences are not indicative of their character—or God's.

CHAPTER 8

DECONSTRUCTION

Part of ditching labels and expectations requires a process of deconstruction. This can be a long and arduous process, and in my case, it absolutely was. I had to let go of all the expectations, judgments and wrong narratives that played on loop in my head for far too many years. And let me tell you, for a label-hating control freak, that is no small undertaking.

Deconstruction, by definition, means you must take something apart—bit by bit, piece by piece, before you attempt to put it back together again. Only here's the issue—you can't deconstruct and reconstruct a lifetime of habit in one sitting like a kid's 10-piece puzzle**.** If you go the route of quick-fix, the picture, the *creation,* will look exactly the same as it did before. I don't know about you, but that seems like a giant waste of time to me. Why would anyone, especially those of us who have no patience or engineering skills to begin with, bother to go through such a painful exercise only to end up right back where we started?

> " **YOU CAN'T DECONSTRUCT AND RECONSTRUCT A LIFETIME OF HABIT IN ONE SITTING LIKE A KID'S 10-PIECE PUZZLE.**

If you're ten years old and you try to deconstruct yourself in the whopping decade you've been alive, then sure, you could accomplish a life overhaul in the same amount of time it takes you to count to your age. But the older you are, the more experiences, trials, and mistakes you have amassed, the longer deconstruction takes.

When we are young and living in the zones of curiosity and discovery, taking things at face value seems easy. Whether our childhoods were fun and carefree or serious and controlled, we started out with zero assumptions about our journeys through life, and we often spoke that way. This is why the saying "out of the mouths of babes" exists. Kids call things the way they see them. Straight up, unadulterated innocence.

However, as life unfolds, we begin to observe the nuances. We begin to see through less child-like eyes, the times when people's words and actions do not align. We witness their reactions not only to others, but primarily and most importantly, we assess their responses to us. It is exactly from this perspective, among the plastic pails of sandboxes, and rungs on playground slides, where expectations are born.

I understand connecting relational statements—conditional makes sense to me. *If* this, *Then* that, statements.

If you do (act) like this, *Then* I will respond in this predictable way.

However, *If* you do not act like this, *Then* I will be forced to remind you: *if-then-else*.

I've seen how fast someone can go to an if-then-else position.

"You ain't got baptized, you ain't getting saved." Those were the exact words a woman in a class I teach at a local ministry yelled out in response to another woman, who moments prior said, "It's no big deal if a Christian never gets baptized."

The mood up to and until that exchange was light. Happy. Uplifting. And then *bam!* The loving atmosphere instantly changed. One minute the women were bonding, asking one another how they were, sharing stories about their daily routines, hobbies, family members and adventures—the next minute, there was a palpable divide.

"That's not what my Bible says," the first woman said under her breath.

I interjected under the auspice of class time constraints, "Sorry ladies, we're not going to make it through all of our material if we don't move on." I secretly wanted to make sure there weren't any punches thrown. By the facial expressions on both women, the atmosphere teetered on the edge of that kind of all-out brawl.

The rapidity with which an entire conversation about love could exacerbate in no seconds flat made me shudder. It substantiated why a room can literally go from synchronized affirmative head nods, with people praising, hands-raised, hips swaying, shouting, "Jesus loves you! Jesus loves me! Jesus loves everyone!" to a dispute over biblical interpretation.

The prior consensus of love is sadly replaced with human judgment over right and wrong. *Jesus doesn't love you because you didn't get baptized, but he loves me because I did.* Really?

The thought of *I am loved, saved, chosen, and special because I did or did not do something* based on what the Bible supposedly clearly states, is oftentimes both insistent and amiss. Unfortunately, most conversations I have about someone's faith, regardless of their demographic, denomination, or background inevitably leads to the same conclusion—confusion.

How do I know? How can I be sure?
I am exhausted by this, so forget it—I'm out.

None of us can know absolutely anyway, so why even bother?
You do you and I'll do me.
And the list of defeatist thinking goes on.

I think that's the part that kills me the most. There is a quenchless desire to know and be known by God and yet, we sometimes throw in the towel before we even reach the hanging out stage.

God has been courting me all my life. (If you don't understand the term courting, Google it. It's a cool concept.) And I wanted to fully embrace The Divine's pursuit. It's just that, well, as you can imagine, I thought I would end up getting left again, once we moved past the hanging out stage.

> **THERE IS A QUENCHLESS DESIRE TO KNOW AND BE KNOWN BY GOD AND YET, WE SOMETIMES THROW IN THE TOWEL BEFORE WE EVEN REACH THE HANGING OUT STAGE.**

When I was five or maybe six years old, I vividly remember sitting on the corner curb outside our house, throwing stones against car tires as they rolled up to the stop sign. Obvious boredom and orneriness aside, I was also contemplating the concept of nothingness.

What if there was nothing? What if that hill at the end of this dead-end street is an illusion? What if that hill and those cows aren't really even there?

What if I am not really 'here?'

What if . . . there is nothing?

I can feel my uncertainty as if it happened yesterday, not four decades ago. In that moment, I had an aching desire to understand the inexplicable. There was something in me (God/Holy Spirit,

Him/Her, again—I don't get too hung up on the terminology other than it was definitely Something Greater) causing me to ponder these things. My young black-and-white-thinking-mind wanted answers and I wanted them now.

Funny thing about God—he's not on the clock. You can't hurry The Divine up like we're all about to miss a dinner reservation. God kinda shows up when *you're* good and ready. Or, in this case, when you least expect or can explain it.

As cliché as it is, my own journey of life has been just that—a journey. I'm not talking about the aging, seasons of life, parenting, or ups and downs in general. I'm talking about the *relationship journey*.

I vacillated for years. "Okay God, I'm in. Wait. Never mind. Okay, yes. No. Can we take a time-out, you know, like maybe an agreed-upon break?" I interpreted, dissected, and dismantled like it was my J-O-B before landing on a full commitment decision.

In fact, since I asked the question, "What if there is nothing?" I have been in and out of relationship with God more than I care to confess. My fickle nature with God is like trying to regulate menopausal temperature changes. Each time I tried to figure the whole "God-thing" out, I attempted on my time, which basically meant, in less than a week. I promised to change, vowed not to make the same mistakes, said I would pray every day, be kind—whatever I thought our relationship needed, I was willing to work on.

If you're wondering when I ended up "officially" in relationship with God, it's a good and reasonable query. You know those stories where someone will recount the exact day, date and year they accepted Jesus and started "walking out their Christian faith?" Yeah, I don't have one of those. What I do have is a life-long wonderment for a God I've been trying to grow closer to with fluctuating levels of effort. Our relationship has taken various shapes and forms over the years, as all kinships do. I'm learning to understand that perhaps that's exactly the point—a relationship with God is not one-size-fits-all. Since God is the infinite, unchanging participant in the relationship, it stands to reason that *we* are the ones who need to break down from time to time.

> **WHAT I DO HAVE IS A LIFE-LONG WONDERMENT FOR A GOD I'VE BEEN TRYING TO GROW CLOSER TO WITH FLUCTUATING LEVELS OF EFFORT.**

Again, if you try to take something apart so you can change and restructure its original shape before putting it back together, and you do it in one sitting (or in my case, a week or less), it's going to appear pretty much exactly the same. Because I was rushing God's process, my mistakes and self-worth looked the same for many, many years.

Growth and change take time. Transformation and relationship? Even longer. Especially for a bond meant to truly last into forever.

It took me more than a decade into adulthood and a barrage of bitter life lemons to not only see myself differently—*but to see God differently.* At age twenty-four, I was in the middle of my first divorce, after getting married less than two years earlier, and only eight months after graduating from college. My life checklist looked like this:

Graduate from high school with honors (check)
Graduate from college in less than four years (check)
Get married (check)
Stay married forever (uncheck)

I met my first husband in college. After growing up in a

small town where everyone knew everyone else's business, I craved anonymity, so I attended the largest possible university in Ohio. Roaming a campus with fifty-thousand strangers was the biggest breath of fresh air I had ever inhaled. I also hungered for autonomy, so shortly after I arrived, I began exploring local establishments with *21 and over* signs posted on their doors. I successfully talked one of my look-alike older classmates into borrowing her driver's license a couple of times a week, making it none too difficult to gain admittance.

I woke up one morning in an unfamiliar place, next to an unfamiliar person. While not a resume worthy highlight, my view of God to that point in my life was *transactional*. It was the *if-then-else* formula. *If* I sinned, I went in the confessional box, told a priest what I felt guilty for, said the exact number of Hail Mary's and Our Father's, and *then* I would not go to Hell. I had to stay hypervigilant, because if I skipped the confessional for too long, *else* would kick in.

As I looked at the stranger who lay fast asleep on the couch next to me, I panicked. My heart started racing, my mind frantically searched for any recollection of the previous night's events. I had none. The admonishments began. *Okay, this is bad. You are bad. Who is this guy? Where are you? What happened?*

> **" I HAD TO STAY HYPERVIGILANT, BECAUSE IF I SKIPPED THE CONFESSIONAL FOR TOO LONG, *ELSE* WOULD KICK IN.**

My mind offered no clue, no remembrance in response. The only thought I had in that moment was, *Well, I guess this means you are dating. You will need to go out with him some more, then marry him, so whatever happened last night can be forgiven and forgotten.*

This, of course, was code for: *This way you can stay out of Hell for sinning.*

I had convinced myself there must be some clause, kind of like purgatory, an in-between kind of sinning for what had occurred. It sure seemed in-between to me, given I couldn't remember any of it.

And so, for only the second time in my life, I began to date a man. The night we met, he had just graduated from college, and I had two years left to finish. Much to my Catholic parents' chagrin, we moved in together, and to my luck, he was a really good guy. To ease Mom and Dad's worries (and save them extra trips to the confessional box on my behalf), I assured them my soon-to-be-fiancé would sleep in another city Monday through Friday, as he began his manufacturing career. While that was true, I could also tell my parents were still disappointed. Nonetheless, I inserted "move in with my almost-husband" on my life checklist in between *graduate from college in less than four years* and *get married.*

Eight months later I graduated, and we were married. Seven months after that, I was pregnant with my first and only child. Six months after she was born, the three of us moved seven hours away from Ohio—from the only home base I'd ever known—to northwest Indiana.

In another twelve months, my daughter and I moved out of that home in Chesterton, Indiana. I could not afford it on my own—especially in the middle of a divorce. And it was in the throes of all that, I was diagnosed with leukemia and told I wasn't going to live.

REMORSELESS REMINDERS

- Rushing the process of re-interpreting all you've learned will land you right back where you started.

- When nuances in people's words and actions are observed, presumptions begin to take root.

- Right relationships are not transactional.

- If we truly desire to be known by another person, we can't expect it to happen overnight. Time is a necessary requirement for any relationship to flourish.

CHAPTER 9

GUILTY BY ASSOCIATION

My daughter and I settled in to our new duplex. I had just turned twenty-five the week before—she was eighteen months old. The couple who lived to our left owned our property and chose the cream-colored siding and red-brick shaded shutters. You couldn't see our door fully from the street but could access it by the short winding sidewalk jutting out from the narrow driveway.

Inside our small bi-level unit, the tiniest of entryways barely allowed for two sets of shoes—one petite pair for my daughter and one adult pair for me. But we thought it perfect for our new mother-daughter beginning.

The lower level contained two modest bedrooms and a bathroom. I used the meager hallway as our library, adorning a bare wall with a black laminate bookshelf. It took me ten hours to assemble the shelved beast myself, using hundreds of bits and bolts. Afterward, I sent a gentle letter to the manufacturer, suggesting instructions would be more suitable with words to go with the pictures.

Evenings, Olivia and I had dinner in the upstairs kitchen. We turned everything into a game. From her high-chair, she flung spaghetti on the walls, laminate flooring, and on me. I leaned against the countertop, ducking amidst quick bites. This is how I finished my meals, while enjoying quality time with my child before our nightly regimen. After we finished eating, we upped the laughter.

"Mama? Mama, where are you?" she asked me through giggles and pretend-closed eyes.

I hid behind the refrigerator door, standing five feet in front of her.

Olivia never tired of this routine, no matter how many times we played. But inevitably, bedtime called.

I cleaned the kitchen, picked up my daughter, and deposited her slippery, sauce-stained body directly into the bathtub. Our seven-step march from room to room never varied. We often trailed post-dinner food remnants along the way, with our family room receiving the most scraps. It contained one couch, a small television that sat atop a wooden hope chest, and a multitude of toys.

My little home office provided an available respite after Liv finally fell asleep. It made a great location for reflection. With uncertain footing, my little girl and I were walking and toddling through the unknown together. Picking up and starting over was difficult, but together we were forging into a new normal.

I enrolled Olivia into the local Montessori school. We both loved everything about the facility, teachers, and location. A ten-minute drive away, the school sat on nine acres of farmland in a large red barn with bright white trim and plenty of windows.

It was Monday morning, and Liv was extra exuberant. We sang Winnie-the-Poo on the way to school. I walked her through the welcoming front barn doors.

"Good Morning, Beth. Good Morning, Olivia," Mrs. Jenkins said. "How was your weekend?"

"Good!" Liv said. She full-on hugged her teacher's knees, wrapping her tiny arms around as far as they would reach.

I let out a small, contented sigh of relief. It felt like I'd been holding my breath all of the last several stressful months. *We're gonna be okay,* I thought.

Just then, my baby girl released her giant bear hug. Resting her cheek on Mrs. Jenkins' leg, Liv waved at me. "Bye, Mama. Love you!"

There's nothing like knowing your child is in good hands. I drove home and began my work day, feeling content. While there was still much work to be done in order to get through the difficult transition, I finally believed it was at least in motion.

While sitting at my desk searching for a customer's contact information, my phone rang.

"Beth?" the voice on the other end of the phone said. "This is Dr. Laura."

Something about her tone made me feel uneasy. Dr. Laura had been my neighbor only three-months prior, when we had lived in a family subdivision with Olivia's father. I always saw her as kind. The Lord knew I needed some kindness as she delivered the news.

"Hey, Laura," I said. "Thanks for the antibiotic. It knocked that lingering cough right out of me. I already feel better."

Ignoring my reference, she said, "I need you to come back in to my office."

I had scheduled a same-day visit the week before, to have her help me with a sinus infection. I was sick of coughing incessantly, but I didn't want to take any over the counter medicines. If Olivia woke up in the middle of the night, I wanted to be alert enough to hear her.

I responded to Dr. Laura's request that I come to her office. "I can't. Unfortunately, I'm busy. Whatever it is you have to tell me, please just say it now. It will save me the trip across town."

There was a long pause. I waited for her to answer.

"Beth, can you just stop what you're doing and . . . ?"

"Laura—please," I interrupted before she could finish.

I stood up, ready to multi-task as usual. My left hand scooted my office chair toward the desk, while my right hand clutched the phone receiver. The chair unsteadied me as it started to roll, then I heard her words.

"Your white blood cell count is eighty-eight thousand," she said.

I didn't follow. "Okay . . . and . . . what does that mean? What do I need to do?" I said.

The phone went silent. I wondered if we had been disconnected. "Laura?"

Nothing.

"Laura? Are you still there?" I asked again.

I heard her take a deep breath.

"I'm here. Are you sure you don't want . . . Um, maybe I could come to you." Her voice trailed off.

My stomach sunk. From the deep recesses of my soul, my body shook. Not fully understanding what was happening, but feeling intense anxiety swamp my heart, stinging tears began to descend.

"Just tell me." Whatever she was about to say, whatever words I would not be able to stop, I wasn't ready. But I had to hear them anyway.

"It's cancer. I think it's cancer."

My knees gave out and I landed on the clear plastic mat underneath my desk chair, right arm extended. Somehow, I still clung to the phone. My mouth moved, but nothing came out.

"Are you still there?" Laura said.

Everything felt foggy and distant. Her words sounded muffled, as if she was under water, even though I was the one who was suffocating and sinking. When we hung up a couple of minutes later, I collapsed in a fit of hysteria.

If you've been through a cancer diagnosis, as a patient or the loved-one of a patient, you know there are not enough words available to properly describe the feeling. Nor could there ever be enough preparation in advance.

❝ CANCER IS A RUDE GUEST.

Many times, cancer shows up without warning. Every time, it is an uninvited guest. Cancer never bothers to ask us what we have to say about its arrival, and it certainly never inquires about anyone's comfort, while it resides in and invades our personal space. Cancer is a rude guest.

Once it crashes our life, all we can think about is how to kick it out as quickly as humanly possible—sometimes without alerting anyone around us that it's shown up, unwelcomed. For me, considering how to tell my family and what would happen to them if I didn't make it, was more painful than the diagnosis itself. The hardest call was the first one I made.

"Dad?" I said, my voice starting to crack.

I rarely called him at work. When I did, it was a quick transactional, "What does this mean?" or "How do I do this?" kind of call. We saved meaningful conversations for in-person.

"Hi, honey, what's up?" he said.

No matter how mad your kid has ever made you, no matter how many times your child broke curfew, your favorite glass, or the law—nothing prepares a parent for being gutted the way my words ripped my dad apart.

"I don't know how to tell you this so I'm just going to blurt it out. The doctor just called me. She thinks I have cancer."

I was seven hours away, but in my mind, I could see his face. I could hear his agony. In the softest voice I'd ever heard from my father in the entirety of my twenty-five years, he said, "No, no . . . what kind of cancer, honey?"

I had to think. In my brain's giant fog of confusion, I tried to find the words Laura told me. I searched for her exact phrasing in my short-term memory. But Laura's terms were brand new and foreign to me. *I don't even know what kind of cancer I have,* I thought.

"Something in my blood." I told Dad. "L something, I think." I wanted to throw the phone straight through the wall.

> **JUST LIKE WE DON'T KNOW A STRANGER'S ENTIRE BACKSTORY—THEIR HURTS, STRUGGLES AND INSECURITIES, SOMETIMES WE MAY NOT FULLY UNDERSTAND OUR OWN FAMILY MEMBER'S HISTORY, EITHER.**

My dad's reaction was the same kind of sigh-induced-silent response Laura had minutes before.

"Leukemia?" he said.

Reluctantly, I said, "Yeah." I wasn't ready to say the actual L word myself.

Just like we don't know a stranger's entire backstory—their hurts, struggles and insecurities, sometimes we may not fully understand our own family member's history, either. My parents grew up in the 1950's and early 1960's, when there was less than a five percent chance of survival for anyone diagnosed with leukemia. There was no way for me to know those statistics yet, or what immediate narrative started playing in my dad's head upon hearing his child had cancer. He revealed all of that later—much later.

"I'll tell Mom," he said.

We both knew I couldn't do it, and she wouldn't be able to take it if she heard the nightmare revealed in my voice. There was no way I could think of my mom in that moment—none. The bond between moms and daughters is indescribable. It is an interwoven web of endless complexities. No matter how many eye-rolls or last nerves are endured, the bond is unbreakable. I could not fathom being the reason ours ended, through my impending death.

I blocked the ugly thoughts from my mind, got in the car, and drove to the Montessori school. At that moment, I craved the limitless love of my sweet baby girl. I needed to put my face to hers and just hold her. Right then. Right there. The ten-minute drive to my daughter felt like I'd never reach her.

I wondered if my parents would somehow blame themselves for my sickness. After all, that's what parents do—take on the pain of their children. When our offspring go through difficult times, it's all too easy to ask:

"What did I do to cause this?"

"What did I do wrong?"

"Would they be going through this if I had done something differently?"

Those internal questions are difficult enough, but inevitably, when outside observers get wind of the situation, they, too, start asking:

"What did *their* family do to deserve all that heartache?"

"Is their family cursed?"

"Do you think if so and so's dad would have been around more their kids wouldn't have ended up like that?"

Human beings want to understand root cause. We want culpability designated. And make no mistake—we want *exacting clarity* in the final answer, so we know categorically how to avoid the same kind of fate ourselves. But what if there isn't one?

What if, instead of the overused, "Everything happens for a reason," we reframe the statement this way—"I have no idea if everything happens for a reason, but I do know I will find out later whether it was or was not."

How many times has something happened to you and not until much later are you able to say, "Ah, so that's why . . . ."

When you went through it, you may have had zero clarity about why a painful situation occurred. No root cause was identifiable. Culpability couldn't be assigned. Sometime later—weeks, months, years—it finally made more sense.

But when there is no source to blame for a situation? Human nature wants one anyway. We often look for an origin outside of ourselves, anything responsible for the hardships we are in.

For me, that wasn't the case. I believed it was my fault. *I caused myself to get cancer by getting divorced.* Sin. Punishment. Penalty. I knew the formula. I wanted to get mad and shout out, "Unfair! You can't do this!" to God. But, how could I? How could I get mad at him for something that was my choice?

Sins were clearly outlined in black and white, during my church upbringing. If this . . . then that. If sin . . . then punishment. That was my childhood perception. With my new leukemia diagnosis, I wondered if I should I even try to fight my punishment, or should I simply take what I deserved?

I had a choice to make. Without a bone marrow transplant, I

would die. With one, there was a chance I'd live. But which one was more pleasing to God?

Would trying to live equate to rebutting my punishment?

Would surrendering and dying be my red badge of courage, counting me obedient with a check in my "pro" column?

Not fully convinced where I would spend eternity if I died, I weighed these questions with the end game in mind. If there was any way I could end up closer to purgatory than hell, I needed those rules and in a hurry. I didn't have enough gall to think heaven was an option—not then. Not after *divorce*.

Only I was torn. My punishment affected other people.

If I died, an innocent little girl would grow up barely knowing her mother. If God knows everyone before they are even born, then that meant he knew Olivia.

66 MY PUNISHMENT AFFECTED OTHER PEOPLE.

Was he mad at her?

Was she guilty by association?

I used to sing Jesus Loves Me when I was not much older than Olivia—was that a lie?

Does Jesus not love children, after all?

In the throes of a life and death cancer diagnosis, these new concerns became my narratives on loop. I had heard versions of these messages weekly for years in churches—or at least, my perception of them.

Gratefully, mercifully, humbly, I am alive today. (I know—obviously). While I'll soon share how I viewed God in the aftermath of my cancer experience, I want to reiterate that I was asking all the above questions *during the experience*. One of the ways I was able to get through, was to realize God is the only one fully without any limits. Me? It took many hard days for me to learn how to live without the same kind of expectation.

REMORSELESS REMINDERS

- Since cancer is always an uninvited guest, inviting others in during the journey is vitally important.

- We should never assume we fully understand someone else's past experiences, or how much they may shape a person's response in times of upheaval.

- Looking for a source of blame for a difficult situation isn't useful. Time is much better spent by taking action, even if it's only one very small step at a time.

- God does not "pay us back" by sending burdensome circumstances our way. Rather, God walks alongside us as we go through them.

CHAPTER 10

FILLING IN OUR UNKNOWNS

Just as overusing words strips them of their meaning, using the *wrong* words to describe each other, strips us of *our* meaning.

I've always been sort of a stickler for proper word choice. I'm not sure if it's because I bristled when my seventh-grade teacher told my parents I was a "pretty" writer (even then I knew the word "pretty" did not signify *winning*, and preferable to appearance, I like to win at challenges). Or maybe I'm passionate about correct terminology because my ears turn bat-like when I hear a word out of place, similar to walking into your bathroom and seeing a crockpot. When we use the right words to describe an item or a situation, it is so much easier to understand expectations, processes, and goals. Further, we can also determine appropriate responses—what actions, attitudes, and demeanors might be best.

In 1998, after I found out my body was sick, the doctors best guess was that it was "some type" of cancer, and most probably a blood cancer. There were only two courses of action: try to make it through a bone marrow transplant and possibly survive or do nothing and decidedly accept my unwanted alternative. Today, over twenty years later, there are mercifully more courses of action and treatment options.

Then, it took fourteen days between the time I heard the words *we think you have some type of cancer . . .* to the time I heard the words *you have CML—chronic myeloid leukemia*. Fourteen days feels like forever to wait for a definitive diagnosis.

I underwent extreme mental and physical anguish, swimming in the pool of unknowns. My mind went straight to *you're going to die, and Olivia is going to grow up without a mom. She will never know you.* I filled in the words of the unknown myself, having had no prior experience with cancer. I didn't even know how to spell leukemia—*is it "k" or "ck"?*

I searched MSN, so I could take a crash course on definitions, while I awaited the results of my bone marrow biopsy to return from the Mayo Clinic. But internet was still dial-up slow back then, and every deafening screech of my computer's attempt at grabbing search results made me feel more and more defeated.

When I did connect, I found the horror stories people put on the internet as cathartic depictions for situations they'd gone through generally less than helpful. When you're trying to remain positive as you embark on a similar circumstance, doomsday warnings dash hope. I'm not saying it's wrong to share; rather, I'm simply noting the importance of exercising discernment skills when consuming information.

And let me tell you, I did not possess any discernment skills at that time. When you're told you are most probably going to die, but no one knows exactly when, your mind doesn't have much space left to make many sound decisions. So, I continued to read.

As I scrolled down the hits related to *leukemia*, I clicked each one, skimming the first few lines of the impending death-sentence overview. I searched like an archeologist looking for the Ark of the Covenant to find a better answer. I grasped for some new technology or modern treatment—any chance to live the rest of my life with my daughter. It had to be there.

I pressed on, reading, dissecting, trying to process the words on the screen, as I wiped away tears and inaudibly whispered prayers of *Please help me. Please let me find something on* this *page,* this *article. Please . . . please don't let me have this disease.*

After sifting through hours of an online crash course medical education, the tension in my neck and shoulders literally prevented me from turning my head left or right. I was one big ball of knotted-up anxiety, only I didn't know the pain was caused from stress build-up. Instead, I thought the cancer was ravaging my entire body.

Everything was cancer. Every noise, every silence, every blink—it was all cancer. Every possible fill-in-the-blank word about the fate of my unknown came to mind. Will I be *affected?* Will I be the *same?* How will I *look?* How will I *feel?* How can I *know* for sure what will happen?

Once I received and understood my diagnosis—once the right words were assigned to my situation—an immediate course of action was charted. My sister tested to see if she was a match and could be my bone marrow donor. Medicines were administered to get my blood counts in check. Daily blood draws were scheduled. Hospitals were contacted, case managers assigned, and other more distant family members, along with *Be the Match: The National Marrow Donor* registry contacted, in case my sister's results showed she couldn't donate.

After the initial shock wore off, because clear and accurate words were used and subsequent action taken, I began to feel more encouraged. My neck regained its mobility, allowing me to look left and right, so I could watch Olivia play. My anguishing thoughts of leaving her and being uncertain of where I would go if I died calmed. I started to sleep again. The fear of the unknown started to diminish because it was *more known.* The right words, chronic myeloid leukemia, could be used in place of the more general, intensely overwhelming words of "some type of cancer."

Years later, it struck me that many people face the same analogy when trying to figure out God. Our unknowns about The Divine can feel awkward, discomforting, and absolutely terrifying.

There is a point in most people's lives when mental and physical anguish over the unknown occurs. Those times and circumstances look slightly different for everyone, each having their own unique bents, details, and individuals involved. But when those points arrive, we search for truths. Whether perceived or actual, we seek answers like it is a matter of our own life and death.

> **OUR UNKNOWNS ABOUT THE DIVINE CAN FEEL AWKWARD, DISCOMFORTING, AND ABSOLUTELY TERRIFYING.**

Just as I began to fill in words myself, having no prior experience with cancer, it happens similarly with The Creator. Considering the possibility of accepting an intimate relationship with God, we wonder: Will I be *affected*? Will I be the *same*? How will I *look*? How will I *feel*? How can I *know* for sure what will happen?

It is important to note here, I received some of the most confusing statements and questions from well-intended friends. Less than twenty-four hours after being released from thirty-five days of total isolation in the hospital, I was peppered with:

"I'll bet you're so close to God now, aren't you?"

"You must stop and smell the roses after getting out of there alive, don't you?"

"Man, your faith must be unshakeable now, right?"

The truth of the matter is, all I wanted to do was go home. I had no idea how to answer their questions. I had never been through anything like this before, I was still very much in the middle of my ongoing journey with God, and as unfathomable as it may be to read this—I was still kind of mad at God.

First and foremost, I honestly believed the reason I got cancer in the first place was because Olivia's dad and I had gotten divorced. I thought God was angry at me and cancer was my punishment. Right or wrong, that was my take-away from what I had learned in church growing up. Sin. Punishment. Any bad thing that happened to you was tied to bad behaviors. (Wrong.)

But there was more to my "kind of mad at God" thinking, rendering me unable to yet properly answer the questions I'd been asked. I struggled tremendously with surviving.

I watched at least seven other people die right in front of me, one by one. I was the only person who walked out of that hospital alive. None of my newfound friends who were right there next to me, undergoing the same treatments for the same kind of cancer, made it out. I couldn't get two friends in particular out of my mind.

Jeff, who was twenty-seven, married the love of his life, Karen, in the hallway of University Hospitals of Cleveland. I stood next to them during the ceremony, their bald bridesmaid. Karen wore a long, sleeveless, lacy white dress. Jeff wore his hospital gown and a Grand Poobah hat to match his grand and gregarious personality. He died two days later in her arms.

Kurt, who was thirty-one, yelled at me the first time I wheeled my chemo pole over into his room, encouraging him to get out of bed and take a walk with me. He wanted nothing to do with cheerful and optimistic—he wanted to give up and be left alone. Something told me not to give up, though. Cancer is a lonely proposition, and when you're scared and lonely, you can become a jerk. I told Kurt so, and decided not to let acute pessimism steal whatever life he had left.

Like clockwork, every morning I rolled my chemo pole out of my room, slid over to Kurt's, and knocked a secret knock. Standing next to his bed one morning, I said, "Hey, just because you have *cancer* does not mean I won't kick your . . ."

"You're on. Let's race!" Kurt surprised me when he cut off my challenge. My taunts had worked—he was ready to compete. For the next few days, we took several not-so-brisk walks around the nurse's station, trying to out-inch each other to our designated finish line.

But the morning I approached his room to challenge him to our fourth race, the door was open. He was gone.

> **I WAS SIMULTANEOUSLY ANGRY WITH GOD FOR TAKING MY FRIENDS, AND THANKFUL TO GOD FOR NOT TAKING ME.**

When I realized why his bed was empty, I cried out in my mind. *Why, God? Why are you taking my friends and not me? I am not better than they are. I sinned and I am still here. You're mad at me, remember?*

I could not reconcile the situation. Nothing about my friend's deaths made sense to me. The prescription I had learned growing up in church was in direct conflict with what I just experienced. They were good people—I had messed up enough to believe I was the one who deserved a death sentence. The inner conflict is hard to describe. I was simultaneously angry with God for taking my friends, and thankful to God for not taking me. *Was it okay to be both?* In that moment, I was too weak to decide.

Guilt for being alive wracked me—even though it was the *exact* outcome I had desperately prayed for, cried out for, fought for. This was my mindset, twenty-four hours after walking out of the hospital alive. I didn't have the ability or wherewithal to tell people how I felt about God in response to their well-intended questions then. But here is what I can tell you today.

Had I chosen to give up and not go through the incredibly scary and difficult processes of fighting for my life and battling to learn more about God—things I initially knew nothing about including what the outcomes would be—I would not have gotten to the other side. I would not live as I do today.

I would not have been able to watch Olivia get on the bus her first day of kindergarten. I would not have been able to wait for her in the parking lot afterwards, her face lighting up when she saw me standing there. I would not have been able to help her through homework and heartbreaks or teach her about the world and others in it. I would not have been able to see her find her own strength as she went out into the world herself, which was the most profound sense of joy imaginable.

That girl—my daughter, has been the greatest blessing and love story of my life. And she was worth every single second of fight. Being a mom has single-handedly taught me what unconditional love really means. Motherhood obliterates the idea of *transactional* relationship.

Admittedly when I walked out of the hospital and received questions about my relationship with God, I still didn't fully believe it could be unconditional and non-transactional. I thought I had failed (again) when I couldn't honestly answer affirmatively that I felt "so close to God" after not dying from cancer. Instead, my inability to answer left me feeling ashamed and confused, like I wasn't thankful enough, or was missing something important that would help me understand why events had taken place the way they had.

While I certainly didn't lean into any kind of transformation with my relationship with God at the time, it was still occurring. That's often the beauty of growth and change—rebirth can happen in the background while you are busy staying alive in the foreground. I have no doubt that God recognizes what our earthly lives demand of us. Thus, when we do not have the strength to show up in relationship—especially on what other people assume is the "right" timeline—God's strength is always enough to keep the relationship fire stoked.

> **THAT'S OFTEN THE BEAUTY OF GROWTH AND CHANGE—REBIRTH CAN HAPPEN IN THE BACKGROUND WHILE YOU ARE BUSY STAYING ALIVE IN THE FOREGROUND.**

Unconditional love is an ongoing burning desire to be with someone, even when they are momentarily unable to show up. Loving unconditionally means forgiving and understanding when the other person might be on the minute-by-minute-fight-to-get-through-the-day schedule.

Eventually, my minute-by-minute survival turned into day-by-day, week-by-week, and year-by-year until I reached the celebratory five-year cancer-free mark. During that season, I grew closer to God—not the angry, "I'll show you by giving you cancer," God. But the patient, kind, and relational God who is unconditionally always there waiting for us to come to terms with both the gravities of life and our existence in it.

In order to love who we are, we cannot hate the experiences that shaped us. Nor can we get so stuck in guilt and remorse over those experiences that it prohibits us from moving forward.

Not giving up . . . walking straight into the fear of the unknown ready to face whatever it may bring, is always worth it. Doing so not only allows us to wrestle our way through difficult situations—even when we do not know the outcome—it allows us to grow into the people we are meant to become. Stepping into the unknowns, the situations which our vocabulary does unfamiliar justice until we understand, stretches us, teaches us, and strengthens us, both relationally and individually. It's preparation in the process that takes us across the finish line of remorseless living.

REMORSELESS REMINDERS

- When filler words are used to describe the unknown, it is out of our own fear.
- Going through the unknown is the only way out.
- Wrestling with the unknowns, including God, is the only way to go and be in meaningful relationship.
- Since most of our questions and hurts come through relationship, so will our healing.
- Not giving up is worth it! You have so much more fight in you than you may know.

CHAPTER 11

PROCESS AND PREPARATION

A marathon is a 26.2 mile race and takes at least eighteen weeks to train for properly. That's if you have already established a solid running foundation. Throughout the eighteen-week educational curve, you learn tips and tricks that make you faster and stronger—what to wear, what to eat, what mantras to silently repeat when you feel low on energy, etc. If you're diligent, you keep a journal, so you can look back later, if you're ever crazy enough to sign up for another one, and most runners are, typically the next day.

When race day finally arrives, you're ready. Well—in theory, you should be ready. You've put in the work, suffered through the highs and lows of training, and studied the course so many times you could qualify as a cartographer. You disciplined yourself and spared no workouts as you faced the slow days, speed days, and mundane days. You chewed, inhaled, and dreamed running for the last four and a half months. *What could go wrong?*

You toe the line among hundreds, if not thousands, of other participants, each of whom has put in the same kind of fierce preparation grind. Waiting for the start gun's shot, you nod at each other, in appreciation and understanding. Every runner knows what it's taken to get here and believe they have an idea of what to expect. Everyone is ready.

Approximately seven minutes later, it all goes straight off the track. Mentally, you thought you were prepared. But walking out the actual experience? Totally different story.

Such is the case for many preparations. You can talk about a situation, circumstance, or event. You can think, plan, and dream. But until you are in your own shoes, and the hypothetical becomes a reality, you have no idea how you will feel. The effort and training you put in on the front end is not always indicative of the result on the backend. Even when you have a desired outcome in mind, whether it's a faster race time or a transformed relationship, the outcome may not mirror what you expected. The first disillusionment may hit shortly into the process of turning your designs and desires into action. But this is exactly why you need to steel yourself to continually practice—it does make perfect—or at least much improved.

> **THE EFFORT AND TRAINING YOU PUT IN ON THE FRONT END IS NOT ALWAYS INDICATIVE OF THE RESULT ON THE BACKEND.**

When I struggle with personal development, I like to practice in the company of good girlfriends. Having trustworthy friends (I prefer some enlightening sarcasm from mine), to keep you on course is a blessing. During unfiltered girl's night conversations, my friends and I contemplate the important things, such as, would Brad Pitt be as hot if he wasn't an actor? More seriously, we also wonder whether some women are truly attracted to the men in their lives out of love or financial interest. What if that guy didn't have money, would they still date them? Picture this as more of a philosophical deliberation, instead of the bashing judgment it may sound like. I promise ladies, we're on your side.

PROCESS AND PREPARATION

I love women and literally want nothing more than to lift other females up. My goal is to help women conquer their world and accomplish whatever it is they set their minds to. I am the first one to say, "Go for it, sister!" Or, "Give me a job to do. How can I help you on your mission?"

But I am also not afraid to say, "Are you serious? Are you *really* going to ruin reputations for the rest of us who fight tooth and nail against female stereotypes by acting like that?"

When I was single, I was not to ready to mingle. I knew what I wanted and what I didn't want. I wasn't willing to cave so I could please anyone else, or to settle in ways that might gain me side-benefits but leave me stuck with a man who made me miserable. I heavily considered pulling a Liz Gilbert and eat-pray-loving my way to the other side of the world. Total isolation and/or a Tibetan stone house held more appeal than sharing a castle with a self-absorbed king.

Months into my singledom, my friend, Carrie, called me. "Get your butt over here, now," she commanded.

"Where are you?" I said.

"I'm at the new restaurant that just opened downtown. You'll love it. The music is banging heavy metal, and I'm here with Bruce and all his co-workers."

Bored and isolated, I thought, *What could go wrong?*

Bruce was Carrie's long-time partner who managed a car dealership. I knew he employed a gaggle of single men, because I heard about them every time my friend tried to console me through another one of my middle of the night cryfests. Sometimes, I sobbed so hard my eyes looked like I'd slept in a hornet's nest.

"Ugh, fine," I said. "But I'm at Target getting groceries and I'm not even showered. I can't stay long—the Hot Pockets and ice cream will melt." Clearly, my food choices proved I was still grieving the loss of my marriage.

Impressing people was not foremost on my mind. Therefore, I had no concern about what I looked like or who I might run into at this new downtown restaurant.

I showed up twenty minutes later, sporting tattered Guess jeans from the 1980's, running shoes, and a fair isle sweater I purchased in college from the J Crew factory outlet. I remember where I got it because I put on the freshman forty (overachiever) and loved their XXL sweaters even more than the United Dairy Farmer's convenience store milkshakes.

"Heyyyyy!" my friend chirped like a high school cheerleader. "Beth, this is Jeremy." I immediately realized she had more intentional things on her mind than the frozen food in my car.

Why? Why does everyone think I want to date? She knows I told our mutually, well-intentioned friend I was unequivocally uninterested in auditioning for The Bachelorette. You'd think they'd let me steer my own options.

"Hey Jeremy. Nice to meet you," I muttered, then gave my soon-to-be-former-friend the stink eye.

I ordered an appetizer, trying to put on a brave face by making meaningful conversation. For as much as I've always loathed the mismatch of words and actions, it was all I could do to manage a pleasant impression and keep my tears at bay. I watched this strange guy from across the table. His mouth moved, droning on, while all the while, I self-talked my way out of a total breakdown. Practice.

Humor has rarely let me down as a source of strength. I looked around the restaurant, eyes peeled for any other divorcee (it sounds French and alluring if you say it right) who might want to bond. What I saw alarmed me. Several young women were with men thirty years or more their senior. I couldn't help wondering about the draw.

As much as I abhor being judged by others, I certainly did not want to project this kind of treatment on to my female counterparts. I was fully aware of my potential hypocrisy as I continued to watch and wonder. Then it hit me—my sensitivity had triggered from an event that took place two weeks prior.

One of my neighbors had offered to help me move a large piece of furniture out of my house. I didn't own a truck, nor did I possess enough physical strength to lift a pull-out sofa, even if I would have had the right transportation. My altruism—now recognized as naivety—made it reasonable for me to accept his offer of help. I figured maybe he had read biblical scripture and it had moved him to extend caring for widows and orphans to helping divorcees.

When we had loaded the heavy couch into the back of his truck, he opened the passenger door and chivalrously motioned for me to get in. I was feeling strong in that moment, en route to rid myself of one more piece of marital property that reminded me of nothing but failure. Perhaps someone just starting out would find the donation a much happier seat in their home.

I slid into the truck and snapped the seatbelt in place. That's when I saw it—a very obviously positioned paycheck in the amount of forty-two thousand dollars. Through a thinly-veiled side-eye, he watched me take note of the potential bait.

I, in turn, made sure I showed no visible reaction. I could only guess the check was meant to be representative of a happily-ever-after promise. Internally, I felt relative disgust and vowed never to get in a vehicle with him again. My self-worth oddly plummeted at his assumption that I would be interested in him just because he had money. While cognitively, I knew the situation had nothing to do with me or my feelings, it triggered doubts. I needed more practice at this single life.

Now at dinner with my friend and her attempted set-up, I finished my appetizer and successfully ditched Jeremy, continuing to examine my surroundings all the while. It incited me to see so many young women engrossed in men who seemed to be fishing with the same bait as my couch-hauling neighbor.

Have none of these women read about that jerk-face King Xerxes in the Book of Esther? I hate to see them limiting themselves this way. Money and stature rarely lead to a fulfilled life. If this was a movie, I'd be yelling at the screen, come on already, move on with this storyline!

The way I see it, unless you're donning work gloves to shovel an actual ditch where clean water can be provided to those in need, digging is a mistake. If these young ladies were going for gold, they instead were opening up a hole where a future of phony banalities awaited ("How was your day, dear?"). I imagined a time in the future where some of them would find themselves locked in never-ending, vicious judgments over unmet expectations by the men who controlled them. I feared these women would make decisions based on someone else's assumptions, instead of who they were made to be. My frustration was based entirely on compassion and concern.

> **❝ I DO WONDER IF NOTICING THE ERROR OF YOUR FORMER WAYS AND TRYING TO PREVENT OTHERS FROM IMPENDING HURT IS TRULY JUDGMENT.**

I didn't know any of those women personally. And I understand my observance of their behavior was 100% judgmental, stemming from my own relational-demise experience. Though I do wonder if noticing the error of your former ways and trying to prevent others from impending hurt is truly judgment. What do you think?

I may take that one up with God later. I keep a list. And if you come up with an answer, I'd love to hear it.

There is also a slight chance every one of those women were falling insanely in love, however, my gut was telling me otherwise. It was red-flag warning that if those women ended up making life-altering choices, they would end up stuck in perpetual remorse.

Concern for these strangers made me feel even more lost in my ongoing narrative. *Ok, who am I again?* It's not that I wanted to belly up to the bar turned geriatrics convention and start counseling these young ladies. I think my repulsion came from watching these women sell their souls to be noticed by someone they thought could provide a golden path to happiness. But if they were not seen through the right kind of eyes, they would remain wholly unseen forever. True happiness is not found in bank accounts, but in authenticity accounts.

Hindsight clarity allows me to see how much I projected into what I thought I saw that evening. I had the Maya Angelou quote, "Each time a woman stands up for herself, without knowing it possibly, without claiming it, she stands up for all women," reversed. Subconsciously, I was living by the methodology that because I had been hurt, no woman was going to be hurt.

Once I recognized the shift in my thinking, my ongoing practice continued. I felt more emotionally prepared to say, "Yes, I will walk into a lion's den filled with single men," because many months of mental endurance training had passed. I was prepared. I realized I had needed to allow myself grace and space to do nothing more than grieve for a time. I don't know if my divorce constitutes a post-traumatic life event by professional standards, but it sure felt like one to me. Even when the dark cloud of hopelessness began to slowly lift, I didn't—I *couldn't*—stop practicing relationship. I had to keep showing up in uncomfortable situations and immerse myself around people.

I now know my ability to maintain a pleasant, non-vitriolic demeanor as I sat across the table from some dude named Jeremy was really part of an educational track. At a time when I seemed to cry nonstop, it taught me I could temporarily keep a monsoon of tears at bay. Which, was a far cry (pun intended) from the hyperventilating emotional paralysis that had occurred two weeks after I was alone for the first time in nineteen years, and one of Olivia's male teachers thought I would be interested to know, "he liked to travel and needed a companion." So, my ability to wear a poker face with Jeremy? Progress.

> **CLEAR EXPECTATION, KNOWING IT INEVITABLY HAPPENS TO EVERYONE, HELPS YOU DEAL.**

No practice is wasted. I've seen so many people relentlessly disciplined during the eighteen weeks leading up to a marathon, only to become utterly defeated when the race did not go according to plan. Clear expectation, knowing it inevitably happens to everyone, helps you deal.

Racers who dust themselves off and drink fluids like it's their job, don't stop, but find another race to prepare for. And when that next eighteen-week training regimen rolls around, they are even more prepared. Their baseline fitness is better than it was during the first round of training. They don't require as much time building up the miles. The underlying structure is already in place. All they need to do is move on from their stronger position.

PROCESS AND PREPARATION

We must pass into every transformational phase knowing training is required. Endurance and energy increase in process. Your phases will look different than mine, but the good news is—we're not racing each other. It's a marathon where we run shoulder-to-shoulder. But crossing the finish line is at first, a solo celebration.

Whether you are somewhere in the early phases of training to live your remorseless life or are about to complete your race with arms stretched for the sky in victory, preparation is key. It's honestly not that dissimilar to having wrong assumptions or labels assigned to you. You can use words to talk about preparing for your future, but you have to take action and line up, or you'll never reach any transformational outcome you desire. And there's nothing like accomplishing something you worked so hard to attain.

REMORSELESS REMINDERS

- If you pursue a connection with someone solely based upon what they can provide and have to diminish your true self in order to make it happen, odds are not in favor of a long-lasting relationship.

- Preparation is necessary to achieve any outcome.

- Oftentimes, there is more beauty and learning to be had in the process than in the final event.

- If you truly desire change, you must take action. No race runs itself.

CHAPTER 12

QUESTIONING DISPARITIES

When we grow and transform, it should not be based on another person's growth and transformation—no two situations, personalities, or backgrounds are precisely alike. We can learn from other people's experiences, but we must allow ourselves room for our distinctive divergences. Sure, we can say we know that cognitively, but we rarely remember to send that message to our bodies. Much like the practice a marathon requires in order to equip us to cross the finish line, our minds and bodies must work in tandem to carry us to our limitless life potentials.

> **RELATIONSHIP DIVIDES CAN FEEL ALMOST INHUMANE.**

Separation is a barrier—a prime culprit in a variety of emotional instances. Think of someone whose family member is incarcerated. Or losing your best friend when they pick up and head across the globe. An empty-nester who drops their last child off at college. A widow or widower. Your grandbabies moving beyond driving distance. Relationship divides can feel almost inhumane.

But separation can also lead to another close relative, disparity. Just as labels and expectations can creep up on us, disparity tends to slip in, as well. Most times, we can trace our disparate beliefs back to our early beginnings.

I made my first communion in second grade. Even though my sardonic sense of humor was firmly intact at age seven, I didn't understand the uproarious irony until many years later, when I married—for the first time—inside that same Catholic church, wearing a similar white dress. In elementary school, I knew nothing of that future.

Becky and I stood side-by-side in the front pew, our backs to the altar. With our toothless smiles hidden behind our veils, we faced the small Sunday-dudded congregation. We swayed to *Jesus loves me this I know, for the Bible tells me so,* and carried on exactly like second grade girls do.

Becky and I attended Mary Irene Day Elementary school. We met over a game of checkers during a rainy-day recess in Mrs. Mudrak's class. Bec and I sat on the wooden floor, legs crossed, faces planted in our palms. We each contemplated our next move on the checker board.

"Do you want to be best friends?" I said.

"Sure," she said.

The concluding recess bell rang, cementing our decision. We put the checkers on the shelf and walked to our desks.

While Becky rode the bus to school every day, my mom drove me to the front sidewalk of the brick institutional building. Only busses used the narrow lane skirting the building street-side. Cars lined up along the exterior of the street. The asphalt wasn't wide enough for two lanes or long enough to accommodate the line of cars, therefore, some of the vehicles drove on the sidewalk—including ours.

I begged my mom daily to let me walk the three blocks to

school by myself. Her continuous non-answer indicated it was out of the question. Instead, she sacrificially waited for me to reach the large double doors of the school each morning. I turned and waved goodbye to her, convinced it would take longer for her to maneuver the car off the sidewalk than it would for me to walk inside.

Becky's family lived seven miles from town. To this city girl, her home seemed an entire state away. She lived on a farm compound named Squaw Valley. It greatly interested me, since I was completely unfamiliar with country living. Well, other than what I knew from reading *Charlotte's Web*.

I gazed around in awe, the first time I stepped foot onto the Squaw Valley compound. It was like nothing I had seen before—dogs, horses, cows, pigs, goats and chickens. Caring for a zillion animals was not only stinky, it was non-stop chaos and disorganized. I was instantly enamored.

I had no idea one's home could be more than just a clean, functional house for eating, playing, watching TV, and sleeping. Becky's house was alive with activity and unique flares.

Along with a giant wooden arrow helpfully pointing confused city people in the right direction, their home was named. Of course, neither Becky nor I knew where the name, Squaw Valley, originated, but we didn't care. It was fun.

We alternated sleepovers at each other's houses on Friday nights. I didn't understand why Becky thought it was cool that we walked to my house after school. (On our hosting Fridays, Mom granted permission for us to make the trip alone, since a serial-killer couldn't possibly snatch both of us at once.)

I couldn't wait until it was my turn to ride the bus home with Becky—the ultimate adventure for what seemed to me the end of another boring week. I preferred to have her amusing bus driver whisk us to a far-away make-believe land of Survival of the Fittest.

Becky liked Mom's fresh baked chocolate chip cookies and cold milk that awaited us. I liked galoshes and a pitch fork. Regardless of location, Bec and I played non-stop. We told stories and shared dreams. We laughed and painted our eyes with light-blue Wet N Wild eyeshadow. It was pure, innocent, unadulterated bliss.

I felt rebellious and free when we snuck Becky's mom's make-up and dumped it in an artistic pile on her bathroom floor. We didn't dare do that in my house. Besides fearing Mom's reaction, we weren't inside long enough. At my house, we rode bikes around the neighborhood and played basketball in the backyard until dusk. When it was time to go back in, we watched movies or played cards. But at Becky's house, where there were almost as many kids as animals, there was no way for her mom to keep track of the small stuff. Overseeing dinners for a family of eight, along with a real-life *Charlotte's Web,* was enough for one woman to handle.

Becky's grandparents also lived on their farm. We could sprint up the gravel lane to their house in under sixty seconds—we knew because we timed it once. When Bec's multitude of cousins joined us there, we raced until someone got tired and screamed, "I'm goin' in!" Then we'd all swim in the lake until the sun went down.

There were no less than four family reunions a year for Becky's large clan, held at the cabin situated right next to her grandparent's house. It was like a guest house, only it had to host large numbers of people at a time, so it was more like an event hall. But even in its massiveness (by Minerva standards), the cabin's taxidermy pieces, small kitchen, musty bedrooms, and lodge-like stone fireplace, made it feel warm and homey.

After one family reunion concluded, Bec and I snuck back

down to the locked cabin. We sat on the stone exterior steps and plotted our break in—simply for the sake of sitting alone inside. The two of us were rarely in the cabin without her family's chorus of incessant voices vying to be heard. Bec tried to pick the lock. I played lookout, scanning the yard behind us, and ensuring we weren't seen. After five hard-fought minutes, Becky sighed—exasperated. She could tame a horse, but not open a locked door.

"Beth, can you just get us in here already?"

"Sure, Bec. Just remember to send fruit cakes at Easter when I'm the one in jail for breaking and entering."

Once inside, we instantly bonded in a new way—we were co-conspirators and break-in artists. Greeted by the sound of silence and surrounded by the smell of musty wood, we laughed until the bright sunrise woke us the next morning. A solid, life-long friendship affirmed.

To some extent, walking through life with best mates is how we most tranquilly reconcile discrepancies and worldly curiosities. Even when we know we should be appreciative of what we have, like my perfectly happy and clean home containing plenty of food and family inside, we still long to explore other environments. We want to learn more about different ways of living. We are curious about other people's disparate tendencies, fundamentals, and interests.

Because of the disparate baseline created when I saw Becky's contrasting home life, I took on a whole new persona when I was at her house. Being immersed in an entirely different setting allowed me to still be me, but to do so in a way that was not reflective of the *only* side to me. The experience helped me understand that different ways of living exist and it's okay to adapt. I loved hanging out with Bec no matter where we were, and adjusted accordingly, with no fear of rejection. Think of the difference in how you show up when you are out with your spouse or partner compared to when you are out with a group of friends. You are the same you, though the vibe is different.

I sensed the disparity in my young worldview, a widening of my outlook, from exposure to a different culture. I felt free to think for myself, do for myself, and say words that weren't corrected at Becky's house. Now, maybe it was because you couldn't hear a thing over the mooing and barking and cocka-doodle-doo'ing, so I missed those admonitions, but nonetheless, I pondered at will. I was able to think about *my own* thoughts.

As adults, reminders like social media, prompt us to consider, comparatively, what we should be feeling: thankful, peaceful, respectful, diligent, well-adjusted—whatever label we perceive as we scroll through other people's thoughts. The perceptions can turn into a long and stressful list of high expectations.

> **IF LISTENED AND ADHERED TO LONG ENOUGH, LABELS CAN TURN US INTO PEOPLE WE ARE NOT.**

Some of us scroll until we see a post that hits a yearning in our hearts. Some take time to like, love, or comment on a position we agree on, while some of us are stopped when we come across an image of someone we believe is living counterintuitively to our ideals—self-imposed as they may be. When we see these disparities, we feel better about ourselves. This is calamitous. *The baseline belief system we are trying to establish isn't reality or healthy.*

Why do I point this out? First, we've already established labels are destructive. If listened and adhered to long enough, labels can turn us into people we are not. Secondly, I want to make a specific connection. Our assumptions have beginnings.

What we believe about anything—a kind of car, food dish, people, religion, or ourselves—originates from somewhere. We cannot decide who we want to become until we acknowledge where our thinking began and determine who we are not. Let me say it another way. If a giant "Hello, my name is" nametag dropped down from the sky and landed on this book right now, what would you write on yours? How would you label yourself?

Did you simply choose your own name? Maybe—but is it truly one of your own choosing, or are you merely keeping the one given to you when your life began? No judgment if that's the case, I know I like my birth name, but I'm making the point that we often forget to take origins into account. Essentially, after the gift of life, a label was the next thing you were given. When you answered to your name, baseline expectations created attachments associated with it.

Gender—Beth's a female. Temperament—Beth's high energy but she can also be impatient. Teachability—Beth listens to learn. Outlook—Beth cares about people. These and others are all labeling phrases people have used to describe me.

I recognize this is a much larger discussion than we have time for here, and I do not intend to get into preponderant weeds, so instead, I'll leave you with one question:

Who are you supposed to be?

We either absorb or are taught that we are supposed to be a certain way. The moment we see our true identity through our own eyes and understand that there are *other* perspectives, we have questions. Or at least I did.

What is the right way?

Why should I listen to the person/construct who told me what I should be?

Why do they think they know better than I do?

What will happen if I don't feel/act/think like others expect me to?

How many inflections of me are there? Can I start making my own list of options?

Living limitlessly requires reflection. One cannot live as a robotic, bootlicking subservient who shakes their head in ongoing agreement with what every other human being says and does. Not only will that cause whiplash, it will cause suffering.

Think back to the first time you remember disagreeing—even politely—with someone else. Was it your parents? Your sister? Your boyfriend? Girlfriend? Teacher?

While the person remained relevant, how you responded to the disparity between your views was key.

How you changed and saw life and yourself in that moment of disagreement creates something like a secondary DNA profile. If you give a part of yourself away by laying your principles down on the altar of acceptance, a discounted version of who you were created to be smothers a piece of your true identity. If your fight to be right overtakes reason, a listening ear, and the heart of who you believe you were wired to be, you may win your battle and lose your war. Through memory, time travel back to an incident of disparity and see if you can map moments where you lost a part of yourself. Once you identify those origins, remember, it is not too late to stake and reclaim the true you.

If I could put this in giant, flashing, all caps bold text I would— you are not what some disparaging person caused you to think about yourself. You are loved by our remarkable Creator. You matter!

That's it. End of story.

It took me years—years to believe that message. I was well-loved by family and friends, and other people scattered across the path of my life. But this fact still did not convince me that I was worthy enough to deserve to be loved. So, regardless of how many times the words were spoken to me, I didn't believe that I was. Mostly, because I did not yet comprehend who I was supposed to be.

My childhood best friend never asked me where I learned to pick a lock or act fearlessly. It's a good thing too, because I would have had no answers or awareness to speak from. The fearless part of me was something I never gave any consideration to. I didn't put a label on myself, mostly because being fearless wasn't even a thing to me—I just was.

Fearless is part of my DNA baseline and differs slightly from my friend's.

When we were kids, Becky stopped short of doing the wrong-ish or hard-ish things while I never did. She was kind and loving and safe. I was kind and loving and easily bored. I think what separated us is that even though Becky wanted to do the exact same things I did, she felt badly about them *before* we acted—I only felt badly afterwards. Sometimes, I wanted my family to be more like Becky's, and I wanted to be more like my friend. Conversely, she may have had her own inner wrestling about my family and me.

> **GOD SEES NO DISPARITY. EACH ONE OF US IS ABSOLUTELY EQUAL IN THE EYES OF THE CREATOR.**

We can spend much time and energy trying to figure out who we really are, while forgetting to ponder our true baseline source. What makes us view ourselves as we do? We often try to convince ourselves of alternative, more plausible measures and standards by which we can answer the question, "Who am I supposed to be?" without digging down to see what birthed our perceptions. It's no wonder our minds get cluttered and our bodies give up. It's a lot to ponder.

God sees no disparity. Each one of us is absolutely equal in the eyes of the Creator. No one is more important or worthy than another. So, if that's the case—doesn't that mean no one's baseline is any better either?

REMORSELESS REMINDERS

- Personal growth and transformation won't look like anyone else's—nor should it.

- Our minds and bodies must work in conjunction with one another in order to reach full life potentials.

- How you respond to disagreements informs how you carry yourself into future circumstances.

- Separation and disparity can prevent us from entering into the next phase of our journey.

- You do not have to give up who you are in order to show up in different environments.

- Your authentic self transcends people and locations.

CHAPTER 13

LIVING IN ACCORDANCE

That name someone labeled you with? Where did they get their source?

I tried to identify my baseline source for years. Recurring questions during my formative years were met with equally predictable answers from my parents, teachers and largely every adult in my life, while on my quest to make sense of life. They went something like this:

Me: "Why do we need to listen to Father Mike?"

Them: "Because he is a priest."

Me: "Why do I need to listen to Mr. Davis?"

Them: "Because he's a teacher."

Me: "Why do I need to listen to Mrs. Campbell?"

Them: "Because she is our neighbor and an adult."

This is what my young, inexperienced, inquisitive-self heard:

Me: *Are other humans more important than I am?*

Them: *Yes.*

Me: *Why are opinions of other humans more accurate than what I think?*

Them: *Because you don't matter.*

When your baseline belief is that your thoughts and therefore, *you*, are not important, it's hard to figure out who you are supposed to be. And when you don't know who you are supposed to be, it's hard to know how to live accordingly. *According to what?*

As I continued to become more accepting of the real me, I often still contemplated if I was living in accordance with the right standards. I've happily worked in corporate sales for twenty-five-years, though my soul cannot turn off the siren call to write. Have you ever felt torn between two things you love?

My manager positioned me directly in the middle, among a long corridor of other offices. I like the work and enjoy the occasional stop from a coworker amid their comings and goings. In truth, more often than getting the tap, tap, tap on my door, I stopped my coworkers as they buzzed down the hallway. They couldn't escape conversations with me—in sales, talking is paramount. Plus, impromptu chumming with your coworkers about non-work events is beneficial. When you've bonded, and discussions later turn heated, you don't want to straight up throat-punch each other as much.

66 HAVE YOU EVER FELT TORN BETWEEN TWO THINGS YOU LOVE?

One morning, I sat in my office at work just staring at the wall. After speaking to several of my counterparts, I was unable to return to my tasks. A to-do list as long as a marathon course awaited my attention, but my focus was gone. I felt stuck—not only somewhere between 8 a.m. and 5 p.m., but in my thought process and entire life story.

It hit me out of nowhere, like running into an old acquaintance in the middle of the grocery store. You know the scene, you're pushing the cart down the aisles, examining tomatoes and peaches, grabbing milk, comparing tortilla chip labels, and grabbing things off your list like that's your sole purpose for being on the planet—when you spot someone you weren't expecting. Immediate thoughts of impending awkwardness, and/or you don't have time to get held up, flood your brain. After taking a detour to duck down another aisle so they won't see you, your goal is suddenly off-track. You can't gather yourself enough to refocus on your list, nor do you have any energy or desire to pick up the rest of your items. You just . . . stop. Whatever you thought you would accomplish just got waylaid—operation fail.

This is how I felt about my writing dream that day in my office. Dream fail.

I rocked my office chair slowly, pondering while I fixed my eyes on the ugliest piece of framed art on my wall. I had no idea where the horrendously bright array of colored nonsense originated, but everyone said, "No thank you," when I offered it as a freebie. Staring at acidic yellows, flaming oranges and funeral-worthy black, did nothing to help my thought process.

I needed that perfect mix of encouragement and insight and knew just where to get it. I reached over, picked up the phone, then dialed. I cut off her hello. "Mom, I have zero spiritual gifts. God ripped me off. I have no idea what all these pastors are ranting about when they say, 'use your spiritual gifts.' What does that even mean? It's dumb."

"Hello to you, too, honey," she said.

Among other traits, one thing I appreciate about Mom is her availability to talk to my sister and me, no matter the time of day. She is skilled at remaining silent on the other end of the phone while her adult child babbles. I suspect this is a first bullet-point requirement of motherhood. I know my mom has a talent for lasting patience while I drone on about whatever unjust craziness I can't reconcile. She helps me work things out when I have a troubled mind.

"Whatchya doing?" she said.

"That's exactly it, Mom. I have no idea."

"Slow down. What do you mean you have no idea? You always have an idea. Where are you?" her soothing tone and common-sense questions began to settle my emotions.

"At work. In my office. Only it doesn't really feel like I'm here. It feels like the walls are closing in on me. Remember that appalling picture I told you about? Well, that's all I've been able to focus on for the past hour."

My mother hadn't forgotten how I opened our dialogue. She moved into bullet-point number two on the mom job-duty outline—help your child organize scattered thoughts.

"Why do you think you have nothing to offer? I don't know about the terminology, spiritual gifts, but I do understand the basic idea. And I know you have some. You have multiple talents."

"Maybe," I said, feeling a twinge of hope from my mom's encouraging words, but still far from convinced. "Thanks for listening, Mom. I guess I need to try and do something productive today. I'll talk to you later."

"You're welcome, sweetie. I know you will figure it out if you haven't already. Oh, and also don't forget the same thing you tell

Liv, "Moms are always right." Which means you have to listen to me—you have gifts." She was still mom-chuckling when I hung up the phone.

I forced myself to go back to work, inspecting my list and mechanically checking off assignments, one by one. When I went home, I felt like a spun washing machine, stuck on spin cycle for eight hours. Thankfully, the spinning stopped.

It's been nine years since I picked up the phone and called my mom that day. Nine years it's taken me to resolve an inner struggle that often confused me, but one I couldn't turn off. How many of us have those kinds of unsettled feelings rumbling at the bottom of our souls, while we try to push ourselves through yet another day?

If it's happened to you, like it did me, I'm willing to bet you squashed your dream like a toddling baby's nose pressed against a glass front door. Denying our inner desires happens much more often when we're grown—especially if others have squashed our dreams, too. But adulting means we have choices, and we have to guard against blaming when we're the ones who stopped chasing our aspirations.

I dabbled for a long time. I wrote blogs, magazine articles, work proposals, resumes for friends, and notes to my daughter. Anywhere words were, I went. I attended speeches and conferences, regardless of topic, so I could hear other people's words. I thought about the conversation with my mom some more and opened my desk drawer.

On a yellow sticky note, I wrote, *Just do it.*

Immediately, a familiar and very pesky question followed. *What if I fail?*

Some things said often enough are truth and not cliché. "Not trying something is the only way to officially fail," fits that category for me. I gave in to non-action failure for seven more years after scribbling on that sticky note, though I kept it in front of me on my desk.

It was fall, two years ago. When golden leaves swirled to the ground, waiting for rakes and smoldering burn piles. I walked into my office on a Friday afternoon, stopping before I even reached my chair. Seeing the *Just do it* sticky note I'd glanced at thousands of times, struck me with renewed conviction. I moaned a long, sad, hollow sigh, then uttered a few words of frustration under my breath. I grabbed the note, turned, and bolted right back through the door. I couldn't ignore my dream anymore.

Writing is hard. Work is hard. Life is hard. And shunning who you truly are is excruciatingly unbearable. At least that's the point I reached.

I finally made a decision to do something about the compulsion I could not turn off. Yet another problem existed in all of my wrestling, ignoring, acquiescing, and finally, relenting—what the heck did I want to write about?

In truth, I had several directions I could write in, I've been blessed with many interesting life experiences. And by interesting, I mean many people have said on numerous occasions, "You gotta write a book about this stuff—you can't make it up. Remember when . . . ?"

Finally, I weighed the options carefully, and made the decision about my genre and book topic. I knew what I wanted in my book, and what I did not.

"I want this book to guide people through tough times in life. I want it to help them with the struggles on their journey," I reminded my editor and publisher.

While I know God has been central in helping me get through inner conflicts and external difficulties, I am also very aware other people may not want to hear about his role in my life. Trust me—even though I am a believer, I still get nauseated when I hear all the "Christianese" speak. I also tune-out when people purport to be Christian, but won't help anyone in need. I could go on . . . but you get the point.

Talking about God is hard. I suppose there's a reason we are warned to stay away from political and religious speak at work or parties. People who bring up those hot topics are usually viewed as a spoilsport. I mean, who wants to be labeled as a party pooper?

66 TALKING ABOUT GOD IS HARD.

It's tricky, that whole "God-thing."

My pitfall in writing anything about God is my desire to get it perfectly right. For a girl who loves words, I'm not confident I can do my Maker justice with any of them. How many synonyms are there for 'everything'?

The label of "Christian" is also tricky. There is a perception—right or wrong—about what Christianity means these days. In recent years, as I've continued to read and study and learn more about the Bible. I've felt conflicted about what I was hearing, and for sure seeing, in Christian churches and circles. I could get into details here, but I won't. Maybe in another book.

You see, for a girl who also loves *people*, I'm not confident I can do God justice. What if I mix my words up or say something wrong, and one of God's people doesn't feel loved by what I'm saying? That seems totally anti-Christian to me.

For the last twenty-two years of my life, my daughter has informed me about God's never-ending love for his children more than anyone or anything else. In one unsuspecting moment, she taught me more than I ever gleaned or studied on my own.

Lying in bed reading the Bible together when she was eight years old, she grabbed my arm and stopped me mid-sentence.

"Mama? What if there is another mom and daughter lying in bed on the other side of the world and they are reading a different kind of Bible and it calls God by a different name than we do? Will that little girl and her mama go to Hell?"

There goes thirty-plus years of church right out the stained-glass window, I thought. In actuality, her innocent question caused me to think a lot about a lot of things. Including my rethinking of what the label "Christian" really means.

Until I understood the concept of grace—that we cannot *work* our way into eternal life (a/k/a/ "heaven") because it is a *gift* given to us in the form of Jesus dying on the cross—my baseline source was more like a "sin bar." I wanted to believe my sins were not as bad as others on the judgment scale. I wanted to believe I was living in accordance with God in the right way. That thinking allowed me to feel better about myself in a way that has zero meaning.

I've had many friends over the years who subscribed to the same kind of baseline belief system. Our sin-bar charts showed a murderer as having a much higher bar than a thief. Someone who gossips or lies had a slightly lower bar. We concoct those examples and soon enough, we have a final chart where our individual bars are the smallest on the page. Thus, we obviously come to the conclusion that we are in. We get heaven. Whew!

The issue with the non-grace-filled bar chart is that we are seeing it through human eyes. Rotate the chart in a three-dimensional manner so that we're just seeing the tops of the bars—and how does it look? Exactly the same. All of the bars are equal. That's God's view.

We—humans—are often way off base. But we can begin to live in accordance with who we were created to be if we stop gauging by inaccurate comparisons or measuring sticks.

I decided to try to come into alignment with what I believe God created me to do. Since it's still in progress, I have no idea how well I will represent my heart for God and his people in this manuscript. Sort of like the struggle each of us have in representing him well in our day-to-day, I imagine.

With complete and utter transparency, I have tried with every ounce of my being to write about other kinds of stories, inspiration, and topics, hoping to avoid making a fool of myself by talking too much about The Creator. But I'm finding out in a big fat hurry that I am just not nearly as interesting as God.

It took me a lot of failures and running to recognize God as a gift, a truth instead of cliché. And what about the gifts and desires he's woven into you?

That dream too close to avoid—the one you keep bumping against as it rattles in your heart? Your grocery store halting moment? You can't outrun it.

No matter what you call your spiritual gift—or the name you call the One who granted it—know you have one. We all do. Chasing it down is the best race you'll ever enter.

REMORSELESS REMINDERS

- Once you believe you matter, you will be able to live in accordance with your true self.

- We are all created with dreams/gifts/direction. Run towards them—not away.

- Feeling torn between two things you love is normal. But it's also a sign that it's time to discern and decide.

- Ignoring internal conflicts or thoughts will leave you stuck in inaction.

- There's nothing you can do to earn eternal life—it's a gift—just like you.

CHAPTER 14

TIRESOME TRANSACTIONAL RESPONSES

If someone asked me how I've lived my life, I would probably say something along the lines of, "However I wanted to." Which really, is a trite response negating the real answer. "However I *needed* to."

In the past, when a label or assumption was projected, I went on the defensive so quickly it left no time for me to even consider if my response was acceptable or absurd. I'm surprised my mom has never hung up on me, as many times as I've called and launched into a story her ears may not have wanted to hear, about some wrong I wanted to relate. I've sounded like an auctioneer selling an entire estate, leaving no room for Mom to get a word in, due to another breathless, twenty-minute run-on sentence.

Without even asking her thoughts one day, I droned on about the offensive assumption someone had made. Patiently, she listened until she finally interjected, "You know it's not true. Consider the source."

Eye-roll. I did consider the source. I considered the source long enough to know they were not getting a Christmas card. If someone assumed something about me—I was going to prove the person and the assumption wrong. Embarrassingly, even if they were both correct.

It was easier to prove to someone else what I wasn't, instead proving to myself who I was.

If we can avoid figuring out who we really are long enough, then by default, we can also evade the not-so-good parts about ourselves. No one wants to deal with ugly truths. I absolutely didn't. *How fun is that?*

> **❝ IT WAS EASIER TO PROVE TO SOMEONE ELSE WHAT I WASN'T, INSTEAD PROVING TO MYSELF WHO I WAS.**

If someone labeled me as better than, because they assumed I thought I was—then I responded in one of two ways:

1. If I liked the person, like friends or family, I tried less hard.

2. If I did not like the person or did not know them well, I destroyed them.

Anytime someone I cared about slapped me with a "better than" nametag, I tensed. I became quieter and reserved my thoughts and words. I held back from sharing true feelings or abilities. Essentially, I turned into someone I am not—either emotionally distant or less knowledgeable

As a woman, I know firsthand I am not alone in that response. I wish it didn't occur, and I will go down swinging to do my part in the better-than-less-than fight. But I still continue to catch myself in the middle of inner jostling between the two.

About five years ago, I found myself in a glass-encased boardroom, giving a presentation to a group of six Information Technology higher-ups at a large manufacturing company. After twenty-years of selling software, it wasn't my first rodeo, yet, to a room filled with technically certified men, it might as well have been. When I walked in, I knew immediately they would not be comfortable if I happened to know more about their world than they did. They were slinging more technical acronyms and jargon around than a college-student slings drinks at a bar to pay for their tuition. All the while, they watched my response, hoping for intimidation.

After I finished presenting my findings based on research I'd conducted with employees who used the technical system on a daily basis, I sat back down at the conference table. The entire room was silent for at least two minutes.

"So, are you telling us that the way we are operating our information management systems today is inefficient?" the Chief Information Officer asked.

I neither blinked nor hesitated. "Yes," I said.

"I have no idea why you think you are better than we are, but I assure you, you are not," he retorted as he stomped out of the room.

It took every ounce of restraint I had not to laugh. Mostly, I was able to keep it together because I value professionalism and strive to maintain it at all costs. But I had also decided many years before not to pretend to be less knowledgeable about a topic than I am, just so someone else would refrain from calling me better than. It was not only my *job* to know more in that instance, but I had pretended in the past to know less in similar situations. I remembered how tiring and soul-sucking it was—so I refused.

Becoming a discounted version of yourself in the name of making others feel better about themselves is limiting. And it is not your job. The onus is on individuals to do the hard work themselves and derive their sense of worth from the depths of who they are. Sadly, most of us have either seen or been in relationships where someone missed that memo.

If you discount yourself long enough in any relationship, you will end up resenting the other person or entity for making you do it. That vicious circle is a doom loop.

My other response if someone labeled me as better than, was equally as damaging and tiring. If someone I didn't know or care for came at me with an assumption in tow, I set out to do the opposite of make them feel better. I purposely made them feel *worse*.

Sadly, there are too many examples for me to list. Like a hurricane, I used words and actions to devastate anyone who *I assumed* thought they knew me. And when I acted like that—there was no one left to resent except myself.

Those reactions stemmed from feeling invisible and being unable to answer the, "Who are you supposed to be?" question the first three decades of my life. Operating under wrong assumptions, I made many decisions which resulted in disastrous and long-lasting consequences. Choices I was never emotionally ready to make.

> **YOU CANNOT MAKE SOUND DECISIONS WHEN YOU ARE CONSTANTLY AT WAR WITH YOURSELF.**

Deciding to have physical contact with my boyfriend so he would love me was naive. Tearing other people down with my words when I felt under judgmental attack caused pain—and often my perceptions were wrong. Getting married right after college, and again to someone else right before I went in for a bone marrow transplant, was imprudent.

You cannot make sound decisions when you are constantly at war with yourself. Could you imagine the leader of one country in the midst of invading another country calling to ask what their target thought a good decision might be?

TIRESOME TRANSACTIONAL RESPONSES

Looking back now, I realize I made decisions with a transactional mindset when I grappled with my self-esteem.

- I will say yes to you—so you like me.

- I will respond in defensive anger—so you stop labeling me.

- I will marry you to be validated and accepted—so I can prove I am following societal and religious expectations.

What I realize, is that my transactional mindset was *exactly how I viewed God* when I made each one of those decisions.

My Catholic upbringing unintentionally taught and substantiated my "only feel badly *after* deciding to do something" method of operation. I can't tell you how many times I woke up on a Sunday morning drenched in cold sweat, then walked through the front doors of the church, waited for the confessional stoplight to turn green, and entered the box. I whispered my sins (to the same guy who came over to our house for dinner occasionally) and waited for him to tell me how many Hail Mary's and Our Father's to say as "penance." *Then* God wouldn't be mad at me anymore and I was free to commit the next sin that propelled me into the same drill again.

Said differently and according to my still highly inexperienced and spiritually immature mind, *Do whatever you want to do, apologize for it afterwards and all will be forgiven—as long as you mean it.*

I struggled with that last part. What did I really *mean* during decision-making moments in my life? I think that question looms large for all of us at one time or another, particularly when the decision on the table is more than "what should we have for dinner?" When a fork in the road is apparent, we know that choosing one direction over the other will potentially lead us down a route where we might not find our way back. So, we wonder—*where am I trying to go? What do I really mean? Is this who I really am?*

I think for many of us, because we either don't know or are not living as our true selves, we cannot fully determine if we mean the words, "I'm sorry. Please forgive me."

Imperceptible as it was, I now know that I viewed not just church—but God—as mirroring the arc of an emotionally abusive relationship.

- Shame and guilt for thoughts and actions (sermons, confessions, offerings, i.e. "I'm really sorry.")

Followed by,

- Big displays of love and affection (processional worship music, fellowship over coffee and donuts, i.e. "Here is your reward for being forgiven. You can leave and do what you want when this is over.")

Most of my relationships followed this transactional pattern. Once I, through my own efforts, got someone to like and accept me, the power struggle and subsequent relational sabotage began.

I am convinced middle school is lousy for all girls. While Becky and I were the thickest thieves who attended Mary Irene Day Elementary, unbeknownst to us, there were two girls, equally as precocious and inseparable as we were, who attended the "other" elementary school.

Chelsea Rettman and Beth Michael lived even farther away than Squaw Valley, on the west side of Minerva. In sixth grade, our lives converged in our area's only middle school, Hazen Junior High. Chelsea and Beth rolled in like they owned the place. They told everyone they had attended *West* Elementary—neither Becky nor I even knew there was another elementary school in town before then. We were not impressed, or willing to back down.

Long before the Biggie and Tupac rap wars, our own little turf battle was born the second Chelsea and Beth walked through our middle school corridor.

"Did you *see* them?" I asked Bec.

She said nothing.

"Seriously, did you see how they just waltzed in here? What is their deal?"

"They might be nice, Beth."

I thought she was crazy and told her so. There was nothing particularly nice about either of them. My girl gut told me this immediately, and I knew I was at least fifty percent right. Chelsea and I had squared off before. Neither she nor I acknowledged it when she first walked the school halls, so I wondered if she'd somehow forgotten our prior rivalry. Did she recognize me?

For the last four years, our summer-league softball teams opposed each other. Chelsea and I exchanging squinted glares from the pitcher's mound. We were familiar enemies and taking our attitudes off the field felt natural.

I soon learned our game history recollections were vastly different.

I spotted Chelsea by her locker. Becky said nothing, I opened my mouth. "Hey Chelsea, looks like we might be playing on the same team now."

"Doubt it," she said, slamming the metal door.

"Kinda like you doubted your team would ever lose a game?" I spoke before thinking, referencing the one loss her team had encountered thanks to ours.

I felt bad before she had time to form her dirty look—though I never let on.

Had I just shut my mouth and flown under the radar, sixth through eighth grades could have been a whole lot less terrible for me. But in those years, I bulldozed over people to establish my superiority—it seemed essential to my survival. However, with the blessing of time and hard work comes understanding and healing.

Recognizing you are not alone in your feelings of insecurity and identity questioning helps you ease up a little. You make space for people to enter your life, and discover the high cost of defensiveness, one-upness, and vigilant protectiveness. Chelsea showed me this truth.

We eventually worked through our hang ups with each other and forged a steadfast friendship that's lasted throughout high school, college, marriage, motherhood and divorce. We have literally been through everything together. Chelsea, like Becky, has been instrumental in teaching me how to think beyond myself. Watching her positive and forgiving spirit in action made me want to change many of my ways. In fact, the four of us—Beth, Bec, Chels, and I are still the best of friends. Beth and I talk weekly, and the sweet balm of her voice reminds me of the things in life that really matter. No distance or circumstance will ever break our deep bond. I steered through many a hard life lesson with their help. I couldn't imagine this outcome during those first days of middle school.

> **I NOW WORK INCREDIBLY HARD TO USE MY WORDS WELL, LIFTING PEOPLE UP INSTEAD OF TEARING THEM DOWN.**

TIRESOME TRANSACTIONAL RESPONSES

Today, I keep Proverbs 10:19 sticky-noted to the back of my cell phone, my bathroom mirror, and the dashboard of my car. It basically says, "Shut up because using too many words causes problems." I know, God must have written that precisely for me, right?

I now work incredibly hard to use my words well, lifting people up instead of tearing them down. Encouraging feels better, right, and more like the real me. This is who I was truly created to be.

Muscle memory often reminds us in an unsolicited advice kind of way, how we felt the last time we went through similar situations—especially those we deemed negative. Whether we were mistreated, abandoned or ostracized—or we *were* the abuser, leaver, or rejecter, and still feel guilty about it, when we are reintroduced to a scenario that dredges up old feelings, we go into fight or flight mode. Mostly, we behave unthinkingly based on subconscious patterns.

Living in defense mode is a gradual mode of operation—sneaking up on you after enough hurts pile up. You have no idea just how much you've reinforced your wall until someone comes along and tries to knock it down. If some obviously well-intentioned person dares to mention your protective tactics, you get totally annoyed and circularly talk, argue, *defend* your position. "I have no idea what you're talking about! What wall? Don't be preposterous."

And so, your own internal battle continues. Lash out. Guilt. Protect. Shame. Defend. Beat yourself into a bloody emotional pulp.

The whole wall analogy always reminds me of the Battle of Jericho in the Old Testament. The first time I read the Bible, after leaving the Catholic church, I was thirty years old. By the time I got to the Book of Joshua, I believed it confirmed: *God is an angry God . . . God is pro-war . . . the Bible is dumb . . .* on and on. I seriously tried to slam the good Book closed faster than that wall came tumbling down. I hated it. I found it all so confusing.

Unable to stop reading though, some passages frustrated me. When I felt irritated, I turned to my typical resource in times of difficulty—humor. I read those Old Testament stories interjecting what I thought was a little funny flare (you might disagree, and if so, I'm okay with that), to help me get through. Not only did it make the reading easier, but I better related what I was learning, and weighed it against my own life. I'll show you what I mean.

The Israelites were on this nutty quest to conquer the promised land (Joshua 1:2). That was their final destination, the ultimate place of arrival. According to Joshua 6:1-27, Jericho's walls were knocked down after the Israelites marched around the city once every day for six days. *Give 'em one for persistence*, I thought.

On the seventh, they went back out there. *Because no one likes a quitter, especially when you are that close to your ultimate destination.* The priests who had been dutifully carrying around the Ark of the Covenant (*2,000 years before Steven Spielberg's Raiders of the Lost Ark movie*) blew their rams' horns. The ecstatic Israelites raised a triumphal shout, and the walls of the city fell. *Sweet.*

But guess what happened next?

Following God's law, the Israelites went into that city and killed every man, woman, and child, as well as all the sheep, oxen, and donkeys. Only Rahab—a prostitute—and all who "belonged to her" were spared. *Joshua, the Teddy Roosevelt brilliant military mindset leader, then cursed anyone who tried to rebuild the foundations and gates of the city, promising the deaths of their firstborn and youngest child respectively. What?*

Let's recap.

Walls up. Walls get knocked down as people are promised and

believe the expectation of the "promised" thing (land/relationship). Everything gets destroyed. Well, other than a prostitute. Relatable? Well yes, actually. Here's why.

When we are burned by a terrible relationship choice, we instinctually put up our proverbial walls to defend ourselves from getting hurt again. Yet, we undeterredly set out on the next quest, unaware we are drawn to the exact same kind of person and relationship from which we had to defend ourselves in the first place. At least that is what I did time and time again—until I figured out and believed that I wasn't made to operate like that.

To say I was cynical the very first time I picked up a Bible would be an understatement. A part of me was angry. Angry I had lived that much life and had never read it. Angry that other people had benefitted while I was missing out. Angry that it took a broken marriage, constant turmoil, and feeling like I was standing on my last injured leg, before I finally gave it a chance to help heal my aching soul.

> **TO SAY I WAS CYNICAL THE VERY FIRST TIME I PICKED UP A BIBLE WOULD BE AN UNDERSTATEMENT.**

Mostly though, I was angriest at God. (No need to scream at me, I'm not finished sharing yet.)

Today, I am happy to report I am no longer mad at the One who made me. Nor am I apologetic for my viewpoint on scripture. I am the first person to tell anyone who will listen I fully believe the Bible is both inerrant and also—simultaneously—able to hold up contextually with our ever-changing lives and societal advances. Yes,

I think that is how big God is. Strike that. I KNOW from experience He is that big.

The Divine is unchanging, allowing *us* to forgive God when we think he must be the reason for our bad choices, situations, and relationships. Breaking news—he is not! I wonder how he felt though, when I falsely accused him and then had the audacity to "pardon" his flaws. Don't worry, I now realize all the imperfections were mine.

Crazily enough, God is also big enough not to send me to Hell for sometimes wondering about a lot of deep, spiritual stuff that I probably should have considered sooner. He puts up with my questions, like, *Is a lot of the Old Testament metaphorical? What's up with the old dudes with the weird names? Why did you make me with a mouth that spews before my brain fully thinks? How come we stubbornly repeat patterns so many times before we finally figure out that you do know best? Why do we run from you, when you are the ultimate safe haven and respite?*

Life and relationships are messy. For all the disagreements people have, I'm relatively sure everyone would agree this is a true statement. In the chaos of relational life, we make decisions, including who we are and how we will continue (or not) to show up in relationship. Oftentimes, when we deal with one person in our life, it requires us to present ourselves in a certain manner so we can get through the conversation without being disrespectful. However, someone else may not require us to show up the same way. And that's okay. It's up to us to decide what we really mean. No one else's assumptions should dictate if we turn right or left. If we show up with God authentically, exactly who we are with no pretense, He will never lead us astray.

REMORSELESS REMINDERS

- When you know who you truly are and are living like it, relationships and responses will no longer be transactional.

- Assuming people have it out for you typically comes from a place of insecurity and fear.

- Those whom we inaccurately judge as "enemy" may become our future allies.

- You can't make sound decisions when you are constantly battling yourself about yourself.

- Don't let anyone else's wrong assumptions of you change who you are or your responses. You don't need to defend yourself against something that is off-base to begin with.

CHAPTER 15

UNDERSTANDING ROOT CAUSE

Understanding root cause is a compulsion most of us cannot turn off. Human beings want to dig down to the why and how of our responses when unanswerable predicaments occur, no matter the specifics of the plight.

From the slightest dilemma or impasse like someone leaving the toilet seat up, to much larger hardships and crises like terminal illnesses, divorce and death—we want culpability addressed. We hope exacting clarity can help us avoid the same kind of fate in the future. But what if there are no answers to be had?

Root cause analysis (RCA) is a systematic process for pinpointing "root causes" of problems or events and an approach for responding to them. RCA is based on the underlying premise that effective management requires more than simply putting out fires for problems that develop. It seeks to find a way to prevent them.[3]

But what if you cannot prevent a situation?

I mention root cause only to say this, from my experience, far too much time is wasted trying to assign external responsibility for affronts we endure. Sometimes, as infuriating as it is, passing blame is not the right call. And I assure you, for a girl who says, "You can do anything," more times than I eat ice cream in the summer

---

3 https://des.wa.gov/services/risk-management/about-risk-management/enterprise-risk-management/root-cause-analysis

months—realizing not everything can always be done has been eye-opening.

It is both easy and convenient to blame your significant other when your relationship hits a rough patch. I know that default reflex all too well. Particularly in the middle of an argument, the words and reactions people use to accuse are pointed externally. Over time, if blame is only appointed in an external direction, we lose sight of our internal responsibility. Further, when an external root source of the problem is not clearly visible, tensions mount. This causes us to shut down even more, and in some cases, look for another external root cause to assign blame to.

> **SINCE WE ARE SORT OF STUCK WITH OURSELVES EVERY DAY, IT BECOMES EASIER TO GIVE UP ON WHAT WE PERCEIVE TO BE THE EXTERNAL ROOT CAUSE FOR OUR DISSATISFACTION.**

That vicious cycle is not only problematic because it's exhausting—it also fails to leave room for internal exploration. I have seen many individuals give up on themselves in one capacity or another, leaving them perpetually dissatisfied. However, since we are sort of stuck with ourselves every day, it becomes easier to give up on what we perceive to be the external root cause for our dissatisfaction.

By the time I entered high school, school work and athletics consumed a good chunk of my days, but I spent any available time slots with Jason.

Minerva high school was located at the end of a truncated street. If you knew the special back route, through a couple of subdivisions, you could reach the parking lot and avoid bus congestion. Most traffic entered by turning off the main drag, opposite the lone pavilion that sat on the southwest corner of the lot. Kids who spent time hanging out there before school reclined on top of picnic tables, shooting dirty looks at anyone who didn't fit in with their crowd.

Jason and I walked into the high school commons area most mornings together—this was like any other day. A voice from the picnic tables taunted, "Hey, J-man—are you going to borrow your girlfriend's letterman's jacket until you finally get one?"

I earned my letterman's jacket as part of the high school cross-country team. Bec asked me to join with her, so I reluctantly agreed. The first time I laced up my shoes though, I knew my hesitation had been misguided. Pounding the pavement was hard work, but I loved being outside in open air, breathing in the scent of grass and asphalt. Running each day after school provided a sense of freeness that didn't exist elsewhere. Encouraging and cheering fellow runners if they became tired, while simultaneously competing against myself to get better? Sign me up indeed.

It was rare for a freshman to earn a varsity letter, and while I certainly was not the only one to achieve the distinction, I was proud of my accomplishment. Watching Jason's face in response to the condescending insult though, slaughtered me. *How am I supposed to react?* I thought.

I was angry on Jason's behalf. I hated seeing him upset. No one likes to see people they care about get hurt. But I struggled to see where I fit into the equation.

Today, I obviously know the answer is nowhere—but when you are hugging the lines between wanting to be loved and loving yourself, and have a chance to help, what's the right answer? I can tell you what mine was at that age. Fix it.

"They're stupid, no one even cares what they think," I said.

We walked towards the stairs at a much slower pace than when we arrived. Silence.

"You're not mad at me, are you?" I asked Jason.

"I don't know," he said.

I willed myself not to cry, while I opened my locker and shoved my hard-earned jacket in as far back as it would go. I needed to hide it from Jason and everyone else, so it was out of their judgmental sight. From that instant, I didn't look at what I had earned with the same eyes as I did before. Pride for my letter jacket transformed to resentment.

That morning before school, I had prepared to make my boyfriend proud. But I wanted him to appreciate me not only in appearance, but also for my achievements—they were part of my identity. Now, he was mad at me over someone else's stupid comment, and I had no idea why he was blaming me. *What did I do?*

I wanted an answer to my predicament—a root cause.

The root cause of relational uneasiness between Jason and me seems easy to recognize with the benefit of maturity. The whole problem occurred when an external factor (loud-mouth teenage boys) slung an insult. But Jason's reaction and mine, altered our relationship.

> **IF WE WANT TO MOVE FORWARD AND LIVE WITHOUT REMORSE FOR CHOICES WE'VE MADE, WE HAVE TO UNCOVER THE ROOT SOURCE OF OUR ISSUES, SO WE CAN DEAL WITH THEM.**

I am fully aware, as a mom to an adult daughter, that teenage "love" seems sophomoric. Adults tend to disregard its relevance faster than we do an IRS audit. Based on my own experience and of others I know—this is a mistake. If we want to move forward and live without remorse for choices we've made, we have to uncover the root source of our issues, so we can deal with them. Not doing so leaves future doors open for the same type of blame responses to follow us for years. I've seen far too much blame inside of families and the workforce to know this happens more often than anyone cares to admit.

Not once, while my heart was trampled by the boy I envisioned spending the rest of my life with, did I equate my reactions to my view of God. Yet, there is a correlation.

> **BY THE TIME I WAS A REGULAR 'OL JESUS-LOVING TEENAGED GIRL, I SUBCONSCIOUSLY DECIDED WHAT TRUE LOVE WAS SUPPOSED TO LOOK LIKE.**

Let me just get this out there now—it's somewhat embarrassing to announce. I have two master's degrees in theology. I learned all about God's nature, character, Jewish traditions, and even some Greek and Hebrew thrown in for good measure. I have written in-depth scholarly dissertations on this whole 'religion' thing. But man did my first boyfriend do a number on me.

Here's the truth. By the time I was a regular 'ol Jesus-loving teenaged girl, I subconsciously decided what true love was supposed to look like. Catholic church and my first love made it clear to me—unless you repress your true self in the name of preserving the relationship, you will be abandoned. When you do not act in accordance with expectations, even if it goes directly against who you know you are, you will be punished. But then you will be loved again, if you *do* something to earn it.

After Jason's affection for me cooled, it was all I could do to get out of bed in the mornings, though I'd never needed an alarm clock to wake me, previously. When my eyes opened, they burned with tears. I lay there, wondering how I could face him. How could I walk the halls of Minerva High knowing that someone who said he loved me just two days earlier looked at me like he never knew me? The pit in my stomach felt heavy. I felt like my life was ending—right then, right there. I was sure of it.

The first day back to school after we were no longer dating, I slowly managed to shower and get ready. My regular upbeat routine of dancing, singing and be-bopping around my room was replaced with silence. My whole being was silent. *I was silenced.*

I concluded that Jason's decision to break up with me was because I earned something—I did something—that he had not.

That can't be right, I thought. *That can't be why. There's no way that's the root cause.*

Trying to figure it out, I reflected back on the first time Jason noticed me, replaying our history in my mind. I stood on the pitcher's mound and observed an interesting and unknown boy on the sidelines. His beaming smile welcomed my engagement with him. After we got the third out and I had completed what I needed to do, I wandered closer to the boy. He cracked a couple jokes. When I sparred word for word, he stepped a little closer. He flirted with me—a girl he must have thought interesting.

At least I thought that's why he noticed me. After all, I was the one starting every play, when I hurled the ball over the plate.

Every, "Strike!" from the umpire pumped more adrenalin into my pitching arm. I tried to read the ball at the exact right second, anticipating how the batter would swing after carefully sizing her up. I was doing all the right things on the field to win.

I read batters. I read offensive plays. I read countless books. But I could not read boys.

Nor could I read God—but I wasn't concerned about that then. I was only concerned about doing something to fix my situation with Jason. Since words were not enough, I transacted in physical ways.

I did not understand until many years later, when I went through an arduous process of religious deconstruction, that my view of God related to the males I knew, and how they treated me. Particularly boys I liked. If I couldn't understand boys, and boys left me when my efforts weren't enough to keep them around—I deduced that God would leave me, too. The concept of transactional relationships informed my view of The Divine.

> **THERE WAS NO WAY I WAS GOING TO SHOW UP IN RELATIONSHIP WITH GOD IN THE MIDST OF MY DESPAIR.**

Consequently, out of fear, I pushed God away. If I, through my own efforts, wasn't good enough to keep a human relationship intact, how was I supposed to be good enough to keep a relationship with God intact? I could barely get though a worldly heartbreak. The thought of an eternal kind of heartbreak was too much to bear, so I shoved God into a box and closed the mental lid.

I protected myself through avoidance. There was no way I was going to show up in relationship with God in the midst of my despair. Doing so required me to risk being hurt again. But even more so, I was too busy assigning external blame to God for the situation. It was much easier for me to condemn God for the loss of Jason rather than look internally for root cause answers. How I saw it, The Divine was mad at me for sneaking around with my boyfriend, so therefore, God took Jason away from me.

My carefully constructed box worked perfectly, as it provided just enough insulation to keep the distance between us. I wasn't at all interested in seeing God. Why would I want to watch someone reveling in their win and my, well, loss?

The fact that blame can't always be assigned with clarity was no small realization for me to accept. It has been both cathartic and a better use of time to look internally. I spent far too many years trying to validate myself by conforming to outside expectations at the expense of my true self. This time was wasteful, hurtful, and useless.

After I succumbed to these unscrupulous efforts, I immediately sold myself on justification.

I didn't have a choice, I thought. The excuse never felt right, but it was a personal favorite. That's what blaming does—spins a believable-enough story in your head so you can avoid doing the hard work of assigning any internal culpability.

Instead of looking internally or offering any necessary apologies, I spent countless hours attempting to uncover the root cause(s) behind my ongoing angst, especially after bad decision-making.

Did she say something mean (label) to me that prompted my rudeness?

Did she make more shots in the game triggering my competitiveness?

Did my desperate attempt at being in relationship with him cause me to stumble?

Funny story. It was always easier for me to justify my reaction when I perceived other people were coming at me. But when I was the aggressor, justification became a much harder pill to swallow.

I stayed busy to avoid internal analysis. *If figuring out that last question requires time, then I will fill my calendar like a champ. I will not let myself slow down long enough for my soul-piercing question to catch up with me.*

When we are in the eye of life's storms, we cannot see the shore. But let's be honest—no one is looking for dry land in those moments. We are simply trying to stay alive as we battle the waves. While enmeshed in situational chaos, uncovering root cause is not a priority. Our perception is that we don't have enough space, energy, or desire to handle what might be revealed.

As a high school girl in distress, the only inclination I had was to steer my own ship. I did not arrive to my cycle of bad decision-making via a map or any proactive planning. I arrived via my skewed view of relationship, which in part, was formed out of my religious upbringing and resultant theological presuppositions.

Why would I reach out to a God who had taken away the one person who made me feel special? I had tried valiantly and shamefully to get back together with Jason. It didn't work. So why in the world would I want a relationship with God who had the audacity to let me make a fool of myself, and for no good reason? My efforts had no impact on Jason's decision.

I thought that's how God worked. I *did* something—like when I said a cluster of Hail Mary's in the confessional to Father Mike and pinky-promise-swore never, ever, ever to think bad thoughts or sneak adult beverages again.

If I mess up, then do the right things to show I'm sorry, you will forgive me. Right, God? Then I can carry on how I wish. Nice and predictable, except it wasn't.

In my mind, I cried out at the injustice of God's broken equation. *Why are you forgetting this is how it works? I mean, moving targets are hard to hit. I don't trust you. Can you please just go back to the box into which I put you?*

I wonder now, with the benefit of time and the reconstruction of my relationship with God, what would happen if adults and churches everywhere, regardless of denomination, started preaching a different message.

> **WHAT IF INSTEAD OF JUDGING "THOSE COMING UP IN THE FAITH" WITH A RAISED EYEBROW, WE EMBRACED THEM WITH A NON-JUDGMENTAL, "YEP, I CAN'T BELIEVE I DIDN'T GET CAUGHT WHEN *I* PULLED THAT STUNT," SQUEEZE OF ENCOURAGEMENT?**

I'm not talking about completely disregarding the sacrificing of animals at the altar (although, hello, not many people own oxen anymore). But what I am talking about is this—what if, before we started pointing out the err and ways of impressionable seekers, we pointed first to God's unconditional love? What if instead of first pointing people to the confessional box, we teach them how to open the box we once put God in ourselves, before we fully accepted his grace? Once human beings hungry for answers know they are loved—*no matter what*—walls will come down, hearts will soften, and ears will be able to hear God's message.

What if instead of judging "those coming up in the faith" with a raised eyebrow, we embraced them with a non-judgmental, "Yep, I can't believe I didn't get caught when *I* pulled that stunt," squeeze of encouragement? You know, the kind of unconditional love where, those newer to this whole faith thing know neither God nor people will reject them because they slipped and said a swear word. (gasp!)

What if we gave the next generation THAT kind of gift, THAT kind of freedom, THAT kind of reassurance so they could keep going in life—instead of wondering how in the world they're going to be able to get through it without making God so mad he turns his back on them? If one teenaged decision rendered them Hell-bound and eternally unlovable, how are they supposed to trust themselves to make good future decisions? How are they supposed to avoid living in paralytic fear, especially once they learn that an unconditional relationship is not transactional, and thus, there is nothing they can do to earn anyone's love?

I share this with you as a middle-aged woman who has ridden the mental Hell to Heaven elevator with inconvenient stops in purgatory so many times, I am convinced it's why I always take the stairs. God is loving, kind, and willing to forgive. Therefore, when we confess, He wipes our sins away. We don't have to keep trying to re-earn his love. We've always had it—we can't lose it. God knows we will mess up. He's not waiting for us like a jack-in-the-box ready to pounce when he catches us doing something wrong. At the end of it all, he doesn't want perfection from us, he wants a relationship with us. Whether we have a letter jacket or not doesn't concern him. Our hearts do.

REMORSELESS REMINDERS

- Human tendency is to assign blame to an external cause.

- If no external source can be identified for a problematic occurrence in our life, we slowly begin to look internally.

- If we have been living an inauthentic life, inward investigation is a painful process.

- Sometimes, either to avoid introspection or simply to get through chaotic situations, we choose distractors like busyness or apathy.

- If more churches pointed seekers to God's forgiveness and grace before God's anger and (perceived) wrath, more people would attend.

- If more congregants commiserated rather than condemned when someone confessed a messy situation, more hearts would turn to God, rather than eyes looking over shoulders for impending judgment.

CHAPTER 16

UNHIDDEN

It's hard enough showing up on time to switch the laundry—but showing up for the never-ending grapple and grind on the days when we'd rather throw the blankets over our heads and hide out? Making an appearance "out there" when we don't even fully know what's going on inside *ourselves*—is one of the most difficult expectations placed on any of us.

Deciding how to carry yourself is a struggle for most people. In an age and culture where image is everything, the choices conflict us in a hurry. We question ourselves. *Do I show up honestly, showing how I feel, or do I conform, and act as expected?*

> **THERE ARE TIMES WHEN OUR PRESENCE IS MORE IMPORTANT THAN UNCOMFORTABLE SOCIAL NORMS.**

There are times when the latter is the best option. If you are invited to a black-tie event and roll in wearing your ripped jeans, Chuck Taylors, and retro Def Leppard tee-shirt, that's preventable awkwardness. It's always an easy wardrobe decision for me—no sweats allowed means I think twice about going. But we know *there are times when our presence is more important than uncomfortable social norms.* We show up for people we care about since that's what relationship is—showing up even when we don't want to.

I was fresh out of college when I became employed as a content management specialist (software sales). I had less than nil in the way of business acumen. I actually thought business meant one of two things: any retail establishment or the mafia. Clueless is an understatement.

Not long into my employment, I was told I needed to attend a software conference in Florida. It was a large annual event put on by a manufacturer for one of the product lines I sold. Just starting out, I could barely afford my house payment, let alone a trip out of town, but I committed anyway.

On the plane, I read the simplistic conference schedule—opening session, break, lunch, afternoon sessions, break, dinner. Armed with sunscreen and business clothes, and not quite knowing what to expect, I landed in Orlando.

After I arrived at the hotel, I unpacked and hotfooted it straight to the pool. *Floridians have it made—golf, sun, and mostly retired,* I thought.

Day one was a success. The next morning, I woke up and reread the schedule. I needed to figure out the when and where for day two. *Breakfast followed by opening session,* I read. *Easy.*

I was starving, so I hurriedly opened my suitcase and pulled out my clothes. How a single pair of black dress pants, one knee-length skirt, and a few tops were going to get me through a seven-day conference was anybody's guess. From my limited selection, I chose black dress pants, a white button-down oxford, and heels.

Feeling like an official business person, I walked out of my room, closed the hotel door, and walked to the elevators. At the sound of the ding, I looked up and saw several other conferees waiting to board. They were wearing lanyards and dressy suits. Long before business-casual attire became acceptable, people went to work the same way many people today go to weddings. Glancing down at my less-than-fancy wear, I thought, *Close enough.*

The rest of the day, I faked my way through, pretending to understand the ins and outs of information technology and organizational workflows. With an hour before dinner, I sat on the long stone wall in front of the hotel's circular drive. My head was filled to maximum capacity with words and phrases I didn't understand, after attending seven breakout sessions that day.

Earlier, I'd barely made it half-way through the morning, before I started thinking I'd made a mistake and would have to move out of my house and back to my cheaper college rental when I got home. But fifteen minutes of sunshine and the outdoor air lifted my dazed spirits.

I went back to my hotel room, showered quickly, and got dressed for dinner. I put on my black knee-length skirt and the same white oxford shirt. My feet were killing me from eight-hours of walking in heels, so I searched through my suitcase for the pair of dress flats I packed—or thought I did. After several minutes of rifling, I realized I only had two options for my tired and blistered feet to wear—the heel-busters or the tennis shoes I wore on the plane.

I wobbled down the hallway to the elevator. Inside, I leaned against its back mirrored wall and questioned my career choice and sanity. *This is dumb,* I thought. When I reached the banquet room where dinner was being served, I could hardly believe the sight in front of me. Not one person wore business attire, everyone sported pool wear. Clearly, I hadn't received the how-to-show-up-at-meals protocol. I vowed to ask others with more experience for their dress-code insight next time.

Every day, we are faced with a decision in terms of how to present ourselves to the outside world. And honestly—it can get old fast. Conforming has never been my strong-suit. Early on in both my career and personal life, I chose to show up in ways other people expected. After a while, trying to fit in caused me to forget how I might have originally chosen differently.

By and of itself, there is nothing wrong with going with the flow. In fact, I give that advice frequently to anyone starting out in their career. It's always wise to look around, take note of people who exert consistent effort, learn from people who are respected, and get to know those who are recognized for their good work and moral ethics. Watch what they do, ask if they will teach you, and use those barometers as your navigational guide until you gain experience.

But we must be careful not to take our self-improvements too far. If we become more like someone else than ourselves, if we don't consciously decide who we truly are, and we end up hiding behind someone else's expectations, we can lose our authentic essence. The real me would have walked into that banquet hall in Florida wearing tennis shoes and sweats. In fact, though I am respectful of environmental protocols, today I wouldn't hesitate. I consider it a tremendous compliment when I run into a customer at the grocery store and they say, "Oh, hi Beth. I didn't even know that was you." I am confident enough to leave my house comfortable in my own skin—and preferred clothes.

Because they are used to seeing me in my business attire, it surprises customers to see me without makeup, and my hair nesting on top of my head as if a flock of robins might fly out at any second. I show up in the office differently than when I am running errands. But in either place, it's the same me. I am the exact same person—

today—no matter where I go. Environment no longer dictates how I show up *internally*.

I've come to understand that much of our uneasiness stems from hiding behind masks—whether clothing or makeup, or a closed off demeanor. When we stuff down, hide, or otherwise force our true selves to take a back seat, we become passive participants in our own lives. We stand by and watch other people's or societal expectations dictate our choices. Sometimes, for the sake of relationship, reasonable rules, or out of respect, we need to make choices that might not feel like us, but only temporarily. They may even contradict what we believe, or we would prefer to do. But we need to actively show up in order to discern what makes the most sense. *Is this relationship more important to me than staying true to myself? Is this job worth what they are asking me to do, or does it go against the grain of who I am? Do I need to decide that I simply cannot do what they are asking?*

> **WHEN WE STUFF DOWN, HIDE, OR OTHERWISE FORCE OUR TRUE SELVES TO TAKE A BACK SEAT, WE BECOME PASSIVE PARTICIPANTS IN OUR OWN LIVES.**

When we don't show up in the moments which require our presence, in the name of preserving our authenticity, we can become frustrated with our decision making. You can't actively choose well if you are passively involved in the process.

Even when we are still running, hiding, or refusing to show up and discern what we truly believe, we are still seen. Our family, friends, coworkers, and strangers *see* us. When we go out into the world every day, our actions are on display. The question is, are they aligning with our true selves? In my experience, if not, that is when we become irritated and off-kilter.

Likewise, when we refuse to see ourselves authentically, we are still seen by God. I know, I know. You still maybe don't want to believe that to be the case. Trust me when I say—if I could have gotten away with cruising through life yelling, "Marco . . . Polo . . . Marco . . . Polo," for the rest of it, I would have. I absolutely, under no circumstances, wanted to be found by most people, but especially by God. Like, ever. Not even after walking out of a hospital with a second chance at life.

The constant turmoil of trying to reconcile my authenticity became maddening. *Is this what I really believe?* Without a proper frame of reference, the only way I knew how to even try to come up with an answer was based on extraneous comparisons. *I'm wearing business attire, so I must feel that I am professional. I'm doing this job, so I must believe in this kind of work. I'm staying silent about this issue, so I must not care about what's at stake.* I got so tired of living an imbalanced life, I made the only decision I had left—accept it.

One day I came home from work and shortly after arriving, realized my then eleven-year marriage was over. While it was excruciatingly crushing, it probably shouldn't have surprised us. In both of our defenses, since I did agree to marry him only one month before my bone marrow transplant, "till death do us part" could have been like, the following Tuesday. Emotions definitely overruled logic.

Now that divorce loomed, and I was faced with a grueling situation and life-altering decision that could have required me to lose my identity, I showed up. I was tired of running. I was tired of pretending to be okay with being someone I wasn't.

I could see no more options to help me figure out how to stop hiding. I had already tried counseling. I had also tried every self-help book known to man, along with many inspirational quotes, along with several motivational speakers' bullet-pointed "how to" secrets. When someone suggested I read Steven Covey's *Seven Habits of Highly Effective People*, I hightailed it to the store. I convinced myself maybe one more book would do the trick.

It worked for about a week. Certain pieces of my life became a little more effective, but when I came to the part about putting first things first, I sighed. *That's what I'm trying to do over here, Steven Covey.* Jeez.

I hid behind self-help books, busyness, and impenetrable, self-constructed walls of avoidance. After years of feeling unseen inside my own home, I got used to it. I carried the "no one sees me" mindset out into the world. I think we get so used to the hide-and-seek game—trying to be found, hiding again—that it becomes a norm. Even if we want to turn to God in times of trouble, we don't really believe that God sees us. Because, how could he? No one else does. We are so used to cowering behind walls, makeup, societal constructs, labels and expectations, that showing up in front of God seems abnormal. We spend our days concealing our true selves, and not really letting anyone who doesn't get us come too close. If that is our standard way of operating in the world, we reason it should be our standard way of operating with God, too.

My marriage came to a crossroads moment. Since my standard mode of operating in my own home didn't work, it threw off my correlation to how I should interact with God. *Do I really need to show up?* What helped me answer that question was pretty simple—I tried.

Talking to God outside of a confessional box was as uncomfortable as trying to use an airplane bathroom for me. In my small bedroom closet, I closed the door—my gag reflex, claustrophobia, and impatience all activated. I thought I was going to fall straight through some imaginary trap door and land in Hell. I not only had started reading the Bible by that point, I had gone back to school and was studying scripture intensely. Once I started to read the biblical account as a *love story with a beginning, middle, and end*, I could not stop reading.

As I tried to talk to God in a way that was more authentic than ever before, I remembered some verse about praying in a closet. It seemed reasonable and obedient to do exactly what I'd read in scripture, especially since I had done such a bang-up job of not following what it said, previously. My clothes closet doubled as a broom closet, so every time I opened my eyes, I saw cleaners and shoes. *Well isn't that ironic,* I thought. *God's trying to clean me up and I'm trying to run away.*

I have no idea what I said other than, "I'm sorry." Those words felt real. It was a starting point. And let me tell you—every time thereafter it felt easier and more real when I talked to God naturally. Prayer is kind of like dating. The first time you go out with someone, you tell them a few details about yourself. Nothing too personal. You don't want to give away too much too soon. There's no way to know if you can trust the person just yet. Also, if you tell them everything—they may bolt. So, you continue in conversation until you get a little more comfortable.

> **GOD'S TRYING TO CLEAN ME UP AND I'M TRYING TO RUN AWAY.**

And so, conversations with God go. The ongoing rhythmical dance of relationship continues. Anyone who has been in a long-term relationship will tell you, there are seasons of discomfort. There are peaks and valleys, ebbs and flows, but there is also rhythm. A hum, of sorts. The noise and vibration may sound different depending on the day or season, but the only way the connection ceases to exist is when there is no dialogue. God sees us from the instant he begins knitting us inside a womb. And he unconditionally chooses to see and love us for who we truly are—the good, the bad, and the flawed. It's not like God only wants to hang out with us if we are wearing our best business clothes. There's no dress code with our merciful Maker, internally or externally. *God accepts us.* Period.

Sometimes we may *feel* unseen, but emotions do not transform into facts. Regardless of how we feel, we can decide to show up authentically. As obvious as it sounds, you can't be seen if you are still in hiding.

One of my favorite scriptures says, "Ask and it will be given to you; seek and you will find; knock and the door will be opened to you," (Matthew 7:7). The first time I read that verse, I glossed over it. Over the years though, it took on new meaning for me.

I started to picture parents and kids playing hide-and-seek. I remembered all the times when my parents worked outside in the yard, and I—an innocent, fun-loving little girl—would run to them and say, "I'm gonna hide! Come find me!"

Sometimes, analogous pictures in my mind of similar situations provide the best way for me to apply what I read in the Bible. It can get pretty deep sometimes, so I inevitably throw back to a time before I had any competing perceptions in my head. When I do that, my comprehension improves. Matthew 7:7 made it clear to me that God understands the hide-and-seek game. God knows we want to be found, so he never stops pursuing us.

In the original language, the terms *ask, seek, and knock* are/were intended to mean a continuous act—not a one-time event. It means ask (and keep asking). Seek (and keep seeking). Knock (and keep knocking).

In other words, keep showing up in your life as an active participant. If you keep showing up, though God is with you even when you can't tell, you will eventually *feel* found.

REMORSELESS REMINDERS

- Deciding how to carry yourself is a struggle for most people. We have to choose to show up based on who we truly are rather than how we feel or how others expect us to.

- Navigational guidance given by a respected person who has more experience than we do is good direction to follow.

- Even when we are still running from self, others, or God—we are seen. Hiding is a fallacy.

- Using pictures based on personal experiences can be a helpful tool in applying scriptural teachings.

- Keep showing up—no matter what.

CHAPTER 17

GIFTINGS

Over the years, many people have asked me how I've gotten through certain situations. Cancer, divorce, raising a teenager, working sales in a male-dominated software world, or running a marathon? The interest depends on the person. "How did you do that?" I'm often asked.

The truth is, for as much as I love helping other people, I used to hate that question. I would tense up and divert the conversation. If the person was persistent, I eventually said something like, "Oh, I don't know—I just kind of figured it out with some guidance."

If they pressed on, I went into specifics. "To start, you need a good pair of running shoes and a way to find about ten extra hours a week."

Once we were on the topic of running, I wasted no time in answering how to questions. By the time I was done telling them exactly how they were going to spend the upcoming days of their lives, minute-by-minute, hour-by-hour, they stopped listening. Any excitement they may have initially had about what they wanted to accomplish was long gone. Then one day, I had an epiphany.

Other than needing to use approximately ninety-five percent fewer words, I realized people aren't ready to have heaps of information dumped on them when they ask about something unfamiliar. This is especially true if they are nervous about the subject matter.

Recently, one of my good friends said, "Do you think I can run a half-marathon?"

"You know my answer—of course I do," I said.

While she had experience as a runner, she hadn't run a thirteen-mile distance yet. Inexperience with higher mileage made her uneasy, but she wanted to learn more.

Restraining myself, and using only five percent of my vocabulary, I said, "Do you want to put a plan together?"

She agreed, and to date, we haven't talked about it since. I know my friend will tell me when she's ready to start training.

When it comes to reaching for an ambition or destination, the first thing many people want to know is how long it will take. Maybe you've heard it said this way, "A goal is a dream with a deadline." Put a timeline to it.

> **NOTHING WORTHWHILE I'VE EXPERIENCED IN MY LIFE HAS HAPPENED FAST.**

But if someone believes adding a goal date is all it takes to achieve their dreams more quickly, I beg to differ. Nothing worthwhile I've experienced in my life has happened fast.

The first time I ran a marathon was in 2008. My time was slower than Oprah's. She has been an inspiration to me on many fronts over the years, and I remembered her mentioning a race she participated in when she was forty years old. So, I checked out Oprah's finishing time before I ran my first marathon—she ran the 1994 Marine Corps Marathon in a time of 4:29:15. I did not finish that fast. It took me four years and thousands of miles to run a qualifying time for the prestigious Boston Marathon. I needed every second and every step to ready myself for the unique and exhilarating enormity of that moment. Trying to force the process too fast would have meant missing out on many thrilling moments and celebrating small successes during my training journey.

There is a two-fold reason I used to answer reluctantly when someone asked me how I got through a life event. One, as I mentioned, I am awful at taking compliments. It's gotten better over time, but it took a concerted effort to do so. I first had to stop using the words "I'm sorry" in my responses—unless I genuinely needed to apologize. I did not want to answer their question, because in my mind, it equated to my emotional trigger of, "You think you're better than me."

For as long as I could remember, when someone asked me *how* I did something, they were really asking me *why. Why were you able to do this and I am not?*

I know how it sounds. Part of the reason I never dealt with the feelings "how do you . . ." questions elicited, is because I recognize the shallowness of my former reaction. But here's the thing—somewhere deep within each of us are hurts that maybe we can't ever really reach. While they may seem off-base to someone else, they are very real to you—the person who has carried the burdensome affliction much of your life.

For me, when I heard a "how did you do that?" question come my way, I immediately time-machined back to questions about my upbringing, grade point average, and athletic endeavors. Later in life, if someone wanted me to answer a how to question, the trip back in time didn't require me to travel as far. Statements such as, *you're so good at that, I don't know how you do it* came to mind. When I surrounded myself with the wrong people, those statements turned into more of an admonishment. *You know you are only good at those things because you practice non-stop, and you know the reason you practice so much is because you always stay so busy. You should slow down.*

I was never really sure if I should have felt badly for doing things I enjoyed or for staying busy. I didn't know how to honestly answer a question while sitting on a perceived hot seat. For many years, my brain fired synapses that made my heart race when someone asked me how to do something. I went straight into flight mode. I wanted to run from the question instead of answer it.

I realized though, that my response was unfair. Not only to myself, but to the question-asker, too. I assumed their intent instead of taking the question at face value—believing they were sincerely interested in how I made it through some difficult situation or went about a certain process. There was still a part of me that felt like I didn't deserve to be able to do whatever it was they were asking about. It felt a lot like when my buddies in the hospital all passed away and I didn't. That hurt was unreachable for many years.

I was reticent to see myself as any kind of mentor or expert. In my hierarchal mindset, answering the "how do you do something" question catapulted me into a "why are you still here when you don't deserve to be . . . you're not better than" stratosphere. And I can't breathe there.

Today, I readily answer the questions when asked. I almost wrote, "readily and easily," but the latter would be a stretch. Long-time hurts are never easy to get over. But they do dissipate with enough time and effort.

The second reason I hesitated when anyone asked how I was able to accomplish something, is because the ability to survive has very little to do with me. Making peace with that fanciful notion was capricious. Because I sat on the curb as a young child and pondered the concept of *nothingness*, I wanted to understand *somethingness*.

I studied the creation account in Genesis until my eyes fatigued. I learned about the various theories: Day-Age Theory, Gap Theory, Punctuated 24-Hour Theory, etc. I got so far down the rabbit hole of trying to figure out how old the earth is, that I forgot what I was trying to learn in the first place.

> **I WANTED TO UNDERSTAND *SOMETHINGNESS*.**

I wanted to understand how I was made. My interest was not in how long it took—but I needed to know what I *am*. Since there's no way I made myself, i.e. I did not get here by my own accord, then does that mean what I do is not fully by my own volition either?

It's important to note I am not purposely trying to open a whole can of freewill worms (yes, I believe God gave us freewill, but I also believe in deep thinking and seeking). You will hear me say this repeatedly—after studying, learning, praying, (insert all the verbs here)—I believe theological questions and deliberations are necessary and important. But there is nothing more important than developing a relationship with God.

Rather, in my not-so-simple quest to answer the sincere question of, "How do you know how to do something?" without having physical convulsions, I needed to first answer another question.

Do I believe I'm good?

I knew enough to know that any ability I have was given to me by the Creator who made me. I didn't gift them to myself. Sure, I have made efforts to learn how to tackle projects, get through school, do my job, be a mom, and even play the drums (almost). Sure, with time and practice I even got better at most of the items on that list. But if those abilities came from somewhere else—then my question was, *am I good enough to deserve it?*

Taking it one step further and adding to my reckoning was one added little nugget from the Bible. "Let us make human beings in our image, after our likeness." (Genesis 1:26).

Wait—what?

(I have had so many "Wait—what?" moments during my God journey. I considered writing a devotional with that title at one point.)

So, let me get this straight. If I am made in the likeness of God, then that means God is super sarcastic and a little bit annoying?

I set out to study about God's character, and it helped me right my askew thinking. I landed at the conclusion, once again, that relationship is paramount, though relationships are messy. And I realized that labels keep us off course.

- How do I label God?

- Is God angry, judgmental, and jealous?

- Or is he loving, kind, and forgiving?

You probably have your own answers to those questions. Regardless of where you land, I will encourage you with this much—God doesn't change—we do.

Putting God in different relational contexts has been invaluable for me. When I need to be taught or corrected, I think of the kids I've parented. When I need to be encouraged or lifted up, I think of my own parents. When I need life-long friends I think of Becky, Beth, and Chelsea. When I need to hang out and have a few light-hearted, non-judgmental conversations, I think of my co-workers and close circle of friends. And when I need to feel beautiful and cherished, I think of my husband, Ryan (third time's a charm). But beyond that—when I need to feel deep, unwavering, unrelenting love in a way that no words can describe, I think of my daughter. For me, it's honestly as simple as that. I know how much I love that girl. To finally believe that God loves us even *more,* is all I need to know.

I live differently today with that unshakeable assurance. I answer all questions from a baseline conviction of *I am good,* with a sub-baseline of *and even when I don't think it or believe it, I am still loved.*

Total gamechanger.

When I saw myself as a gift, I went back to an early question I wrestled with. *How was I made?*

You may know exactly what I'm talking about. Is there some stirring deep within you that you can't shake? Inherent abilities you enjoy, perhaps precipitating your friends to ask, "How do you do that?"

Calling is a funny word to me. The first time I heard someone use it in the context of a gift from God, my sarcasm took over. *Like, E.T. phoning home kind of calling? God is phoning Earth from Heaven?*

I'm telling you—when I say I went kicking and screaming over anything God-related, I am not embellishing for effect.

I knew what it meant then, and I know what it means now. And I know you do, too. That thing you can't stop thinking about? The gnawing voice in your head that says, *You should teach . . . you should open your own shop . . . you should start a nonprofit. . . .*

> **WE OFTEN WONDER HOW WE CAN TELL THE DIFFERENCE BETWEEN OUR LIKES AND INTERESTS VERSUS OUR *CALLINGS*—THE MAGNETISM OF THE DRAW PROVIDES A CLUE.**

Those thoughts are in your heart for a reason. *They are calling you back to how and why you were made.* We often wonder how we can tell the difference between our likes and interests versus our *callings*—the magnetism of the draw provides a clue.

You were made as a gift. You are a gift. And, you have a gift.

How are you using yours?

The harder you try to silence, outrun, or avoid your God-given talent—the more it lures you back. Callings cannot be ignored. Trust me—I tried. It took me several years to ask for a sabbatical from my day-job so I could write this book. Along the way, people said, "You have a gift." But I dismissed their words and shushed them away.

If someone gave me a compliment, I said, "I'm not listening to you. No thanks. No one is home. Can't take the call."

After twenty-five years of enjoying a successful career, do you know how long it took me to adjust to my sabbatical? Two days. I've not thought about the job once. That's telling. Sure, I miss some of my friends, but they didn't go anywhere. I did. I took the call—the one for which I was made.

I'm convinced the ways God works cannot be fully explained. People have tried. The Bible tells us all we need and were meant to know. I am grateful for both the words and the Word. But I can tell you this, based on my own journey and experience, I will never, ever have enough words or gratitude to explain everything—*as in, the everything eternal God.*

And that's my favorite gift of all.

GIFTINGS

REMORSELESS REMINDERS

- You can't force-feed ideas or answers to people—especially when the subject matter relates to something they are inexperienced with or fearful of (i.e. God/church/religion).

- Everyone is made with a gift inside. Whether we choose to see it or use it is always up to us.

- Answering "the call" looks different for everyone—as it should. We are unique, as are the gifts we have been given.

- It's possible your gift has not been turned into a calling because it is not being used for the benefit of others.

CHAPTER 18

WALK DON'T RUN

Along with strong endings to books and movies, I love good quotes. If my high school American literature teacher had told me Mark Twain said, "Good judgement is the result of experience, and experience is the result of bad judgment," I would have paid more attention in class.

It can be hard to notice signs and indicators that we are growing closer in alignment with our true selves. They can vary and are often subtle. Generally, the clues unfold over time, but ongoing experience is the primary requirement for our transformation. While it would be convenient to stumble upon a *Congratulations! You are now the person you were created to be!* announcement while scrolling through social media, I'm convinced the process is not supposed to work that way. Rather, we learn as we go.

It is impossible to obtain the necessary wisdom required to accept ourselves as designed, without walking through circumstances. Because showing up as an active participant in life is a prerequisite, finding ourselves along the way becomes a treasured byproduct.

We should expect proverbial bumps in the road when we choose not to show up and make the trek on our self-acceptance journeys. I tripped over my share of bumpy terrain while trying to avoid what seemed like agonizing work to live fully as the real me—detours are always readily available.

I chose various cloaks to hide under while I remained in the comforts of my own selfishness. When I ran from God, indifference was my staple camouflage. And I layered in other accessories to adorn my disguise: busyness, skepticism, bitterness and distrust. If I thought the chances of disappointment or abandonment were high in any kind of relationship—I added more covering—until something strange happened.

> **ONCE I BEGAN TO BELIEVE GOD FORGAVE ME, A SHIFTING BEGAN.**

I amassed a copious amount of experience as the result of my bad judgements, but once I began to believe God forgave me, a shifting began. I started weighing present circumstances against prior situations and outcomes, then considered my choices in light of my past results. My judgement improved, and when I chose more wisely, my self-confidence increased.

A week after I decided I was going to the convent instead of dating again, one of my long-time customers emailed me. *Beth, I have a friend who lives in Louisville, Kentucky. He is coming up to visit me for the weekend and I'd like you to meet him.*

Delete.

I typed on my laptop from the comfort of my bed, leaning against the beige fabric headboard. Leftover pizza and a half-eaten quart of ice cream rested against a stack of books on my nightstand—dinner in the kitchen seemed too normal during that season of my life. With the small wall-mounted television on for background noise, I was in the middle of typing another email when the phone rang.

"Hello there, why did you not respond to my email?" my

customer said. "I know you saw it—you always respond within minutes."

"Please don't bug me about this," I said.

I silently considered how I would spin my default "I'm not ready to date," excuse. Not that she would listen. My customer was aware I hadn't been in a serious relationship for three years—and she was pushier than me.

"You're going. It's been a while since I have seen him, but from what I remember, you two have a lot in common," she said.

After a few minutes of going back and forth, I knew it was futile to resist, so I reluctantly agreed with one stipulation. I would go out with this guy once, and she was coming with us.

The blind date weekend arrived. I met the two of them, along with five of their mutual friends, at the local bowling alley. I was relieved when I walked in and saw the others. The more people, the less chance for any awkwardness. When my customer suggested a night of bowling over the phone, I didn't argue. *I can wear jeans and an old flannel. Maybe it won't be so bad,* I thought.

Wrong.

I was no dating connoisseur, but I knew proper etiquette dictated getting to know someone before acting like you'd known them forever. My *date* did not understand the protocol.

"She'll have the pizza," the man from Kentucky said to the waitress.

"Thanks, but no I won't. I had pizza last night," I said.

He forced a smile. I excused myself to the restroom.

Standing in front of the mirror, I talked myself out of leaving. Then I sent a text to my customer telling her that her future purchase prices had just tripled.

Since dating requires effort, I composed myself and went back out and joined the other bowlers. After an honest attempt at conversation, including listening to my date's antipathy for running—I knew I would not be going to the Kentucky Derby anytime soon. We were not compatible.

The night finally ended, and I bid a lightning fast farewell to the group. On my drive home, it dawned on me—the pain and suffering I had gone through when my marriage ended didn't go to waste. I smiled, remembering the look on Mr. Kentuckian's face when I outpaced him as I exited. *Okay, there was no way you were going to miss those signs.*

I high-fived myself. Not only had I recognized the mismatch warnings, but more importantly, I didn't ignore them this time.

It took me years to believe I was even worthy of walking through future experiences without repeating previous mistakes. For a long time, since I had not forgiven myself for past decisions, I stayed stuck living under the false notion that God had not forgiven me either. It wasn't until I showed up as my authentic self with God that I understood otherwise.

I had to *experience* the intimate relational equation with God—instead of operating as if the formula others had *told* me made sense. And do you know what I finally figured out other than I hate math? The relational equation is not *if/then*. It's *when/always*.

When you ask to be forgiven for all the disastrous choices you've made, God always says, "yes." There is no hesitation. There is no catch. There is no fine-print clause. It's just, "You are forgiven because I love you."

Exercising patience is often a difficulty people face as the processes of self-acceptance and a relationship with God unfold. I know it certainly was for me. Patience was never my natural tendency. I was even worse at submission. I tried to segregate what I saw in the world around me and what a relationship with God could look like.

You know those bumper stickers that say, *Don't let the car fool you, my treasure is in heaven*? Well, I stopped rolling my eyes at that message once I understood what it really meant.

We are the ones fooling ourselves if we think our treasures are only what we see right in front of us. Living under that premise is understandable, if not logical. We wake up and go about our business "in the world." Our culture informs how that should look.

Society programs us from a very early age that we must attain the next reward and get the prize. When we are children, it looks something like this, *If you eat all your vegetables, you can stay up a few minutes later tonight.* The older we become, the higher the stakes. *If you get a good job, you can buy a house . . . if you get a better job, you can buy a bigger house.* Satisfaction is elusive, especially when we compare it to the wrong benchmark.

I operated under the get a prize criterion for many years. I strived to reach some fleeting destination, hoping for a final arrival. Because I hadn't experienced an alternative, I didn't know functioning that way was not in my best interest. It wasn't until I took my disguises off and started hanging out with God in my real skin, that I started to understand more clearly. Early on, I knew I needed to learn more, so I went back to scripture and started reading.

What's ironic to me now, is that I initially dismissed the first thirty-nine books of the Bible because I thought the people referenced in the Old Testament were clueless about today's issues. I know—it was short-sighted. As it turned out, when I was more patient with the reading process and went back to the beginning of the Bible, new discoveries came to light. I became particularly fond of King David. There was no question who owned the biggest house back in the day.

During his kingship, David acquired incredible wealth. His goal was to build the Temple as a resting place for God. Even though his son, Solomon, ended up following through on the Temple's construction, David donated his entire estate to that purpose. By today's standards, some estimates calculate King David's monetary worth in the five to ten-billion-dollar range. And yet—his satisfaction waned.

King David was always a man after God's own heart (1 Samuel 13:14, Acts 13:22). But when he started acting contrary to God's design, he started making grievous decisions. From lying and cheating to murder, King David covered some sinful doozies. Does that mean he wasn't forgiven? No.

> **WHEN YOU STOP RUNNING FROM GOD, YOU CAN START WALKING THROUGH LIFE EXPERIENCES IN A WHOLE NEW WAY.**

God forgave David just as he forgives anyone who asks. But David had consequences, because he ignored the signs meant to keep him in alignment with his true self. This threw him off course, causing a fatal outcome. We would be wise to learn from King David's mistake.

When you stop running from God, you can start walking through life experiences in a whole new way. You'll no longer feel the need to show up like it's Halloween, dressed as a super-secret covert spy. Your mindset will shift, allowing you to recognize that real relationships, and accepting your true self within them, requires investments of energy, time, and endurance.

No relationship has taught me more about how God sees us than in my role as a parent. I loved my daughter unconditionally the second she was born. And yet, inexplicable as it is to me, my love for her has deepened immeasurably over the last twenty-two years. When she was little, she viewed me as invincible. Her every question about life, I answered. When she was little, I could have told her the sky was red instead of blue and she would have believed me.

As my baby girl grew up though, she encountered additional frames of references. I became a little less believable. She had questions. Because I loved her, I relentlessly tried to teach her the ways I thought best. As she grew up, however, she rejected some of my teachings. She wanted to learn on her own.

At the same time my daughter was experiencing (testing) what I had always told her, something else was happening—I accepted my need to let her find her own way. As she pulled back from me, I gave her the space to do so. Being momentarily out of relationship with her was brutal. I cried myself to sleep most nights, even though I never let her see how much she was breaking my heart.

Friends and family encouraged me, "She'll be back," they said. But I wasn't even sure where she had gone.

My daughter went on her own journey. She had to walk through circumstances experientially—instead of following me, as I told her how everything was supposed to be done. She had to show up authentically in her own life and make the trek, traversing into unfamiliar territories. She came out on the other side as her treasured, true self. And, it took her much less time than it did me, I might add.

Watching my baby grow into the person she was created to be has been the greatest joy in my life. Because we experience a disguise-free relationship together, I am convinced our unbreakable bond is everlasting. No one can tell me otherwise. She and I walk through the intimacy of our relationship's highs and lows, ebbs and flows, heart-to-heart. We ask and offer forgiveness. Our connection continues to strengthen. I can't imagine an existence in which our bi-directional love stops. I have neither the means nor the desire to undo what is true. I loved her unconditionally when she was born, I love her unconditionally now, and I will love her unconditionally always.

The same cannot be said about God. You read that right.

God loves us even more. There are no words to describe God's amazing, unfailing adoration. There just aren't.

For as much as we have been conditioned to believe otherwise, there also aren't any words to fully describe you or me. We have been given birth names, nicknames, surnames, titles, and brands. We have been assigned birth order, importance, rankings, and (social-media) likes. And we have been expected to both accept and live up to those descriptions.

> **THERE ARE NO WORDS TO DESCRIBE GOD'S AMAZING, UNFAILING ADORATION. THERE JUST AREN'T.**

Except here's the thing—*when we answer to labels, our life pictures cannot be fully painted.* We are incomplete works of art left hanging in the wrong gallery, awaiting the proper inscription. Authenticity means only we get to choose what is written.

I remain convinced that whatever label you were wrongly assigned is exactly the expectation you have been trying to defy ever since. In King David's case, he was labeled as a "great conqueror." As such, he often found himself involved in intense warfare and power struggles. Instead, he would much rather have devoted himself to the desire so deeply embedded in his heart, of building a temple for God.

When David was at the top—King of the entire Mediterranean region—he made choices in direct opposition of who he truly was. David's real self was a man after God's own heart.

When you run toward a bigger kingdom, title, reward—whatever external expectation that isn't in alignment with who you were created to be—you walk away from yourself. Running toward the illusion of, "there's always more to prove so I can slay this label," precludes us from remembering Jesus' walk and final utterance. "It is finished," means just that, he was able to provide exactly what we needed. Completely.

> **THERE IS NOTHING MORE FOR US TO DO—OTHER THAN SHOW UP AS OUR AUTHENTIC, MESSY SELVES AND HAVE A REAL RELATIONSHIP WITH GOD.**

For all the times I stayed trapped in guilt, for all the times I hid the honesty of who I am, for all the times I said, "I'm not a very good Christian," I now finally understand. There is nothing more for us to do—other than show up as our authentic, messy selves and have a real relationship with God.

Doing so will bring about the most profound sense of freedom you can imagine. You will no longer walk into a room and wonder if you should be there. You will no longer wonder what others are whispering about. You will no longer feel the need to conform to beliefs about yourself that are untrue. You will no longer settle for less than you deserve. And you will no longer—under any circumstance—need to hide.

Instead, you will be free to show up and walk out the rest of your life exactly how you were created to. Remorselessly.

CONCLUSION

You've read the stories in this book, and now know more about me than I ever wanted another human being to know. Congratulations! I feel like such a sucker.

Now that we're officially friends, I want to ask you something very important. Do you feel like the real you?

It can be a tough question to answer without sounding flippant. For many of us, life is pretty good—no major losses at the moment, no illnesses to speak of, nothing to write home about. Wondering who you truly are in times of relative peace may not be something you consider at all. However, when life gets messy—divorce, disease, death—the question, "What is the point of any of this?" often arises. And usually, it is exactly within that vat of transitional despair when we seek to uncover who we really are.

Truth be told, I am right smack dab in the middle of that ongoing uncovering, again. *Hey, write what you know, right?*

My continuing relationship with God has continued to reveal and confirm who I have always been. All good there. Nothing too new to report (finally). However, now that I have done the hard work required to ditch inaccurate labels, expectations, and assumptions about myself, I find myself wondering, *What am I going to do with this newfound acceptance through my intimate relationship with God?*

Six months ago, I approached the decision-makers of the

company where I've been employed for the last twenty-three years. "What do you think about the idea of me taking a sabbatical?" I said.

The words spoken in response were positive, but I could tell by the look on their faces they didn't think I was serious. After all, I sometimes spew crazy ideas at warp speed. But after the words came out of my mouth, I spent the next month asking myself how serious I was.

I couldn't talk myself out of it. The following month, I began a nine-month sabbatical to pursue a dream that has chased me for a lifetime. I write to you here, now, on the anniversary of month two. I've always known I had a heart for God. But after doing a fairly decent job of pretending I didn't, I could no longer outrun *his* heart's call.

I am a lover of words (please insert a surprised face emoji here), and a lover of people. I told you both of those things about myself already. Any time I repressed either tug, it was at the expense of the real me. So, when I stepped away from my day job for this sabbatical, I chose to use my time in the most vulnerable way possible—as my true self.

I decided to write this book after attending a local writing and speaking conference. The people I met during the two-day event were inspiring, courageous, and living lives that mirrored who they knew God created them to be. Shortly after the conference ended, I reconnected with one of the women I met, asking for guidance on my writing journey. I had no idea what I was doing.

When she explained there was an option to work with her and an editor (read: book doctor/magic-maker) in an abbreviated amount of time to bring my book to life—I did not hesitate. "I'm in!" I told her.

CONCLUSION

Five-weeks after I made the decision to move forward, I arrived at her retreat space and began writing seventeen to eighteen hours a day, non-stop. No exaggeration! I have pictures with my raccoon eyes to prove it.

Here's what I want you to know. I was adamant—as in, unwaveringly stubborn—that I was not going to overtly write about God. Less than ten minutes after we dropped our suitcases and settled in, we sat down to work. The very first words out of my mouth were not pleasantries. "This will not be a Christian book," I said. "I hate labels. I would prefer this book doesn't get one."

Both my publisher and editor smiled and shook their heads in affirmation at my pronouncement, and we dug in. I showed them what I had written. We mapped out potential direction. We discussed a book title and chapter titles.

By the second full day of writing, my publisher said, "You know you can't go five minutes without talking about God, right?"

I laughed when she said it, and I am laughing now as I share it with you, less than a week after returning home. How you show up in the world is an ongoing process. How you show up in relationship is an ongoing process. *Our stories are an ongoing process.* Just because you figure out who you were created to be does not mean instant comfort as you try to live your life in a way that matches God's design. Nor does it mean you will always know, directionally, exactly where to go at the outset. And it *definitely* doesn't guarantee your outcome will look precisely like you or anyone else expected. But being remorseless means living without shame in spite of wrongdoing or temporary detours. Living remorselessly means bravely forging on, and never giving up, while you discover God's plans. It means refusing to lose yourself and choosing a beautiful, unapologetic, and passionate yes to your on purpose design.

The real you is perfectly enough. God made your authentic self exactly as he intended. He expects you to be amazing and assumes you are wonderful, because you are. As you continue on your journey, may you always know and remember there is only one nametag that matters—loved.

That's one label no one can ever take away.

ABOUT THE AUTHOR

Beth Fisher has been in sales for almost three decades, working with a myriad of organizations and people alike. Her strong business acumen coupled with her passionate desire to help others traverse difficult life journeys is what led Beth to recently resign from the corporate world and pursue her calling. She now serves as Vice President of Advancement for Mel Trotter Ministries—a non-profit organization which exists to demonstrate the compassion of Jesus Christ through rescue and restoration for anyone experiencing homelessness.

In addition, Beth's passion to help others on their journeys is what inspired her to become an entrepreneur. In conjunction with her organization, Leave It 2 B, Beth serves individuals through transformational 1:1 and group coaching and motivational corporate leadership speaking and training.

An avid marathoner and two-time Boston Marathon qualifier, Beth lives in Grand Rapids, Michigan with her husband, Ryan, and daughter, Olivia.

CONNECT WITH THE AUTHOR

www.bethfisher.com
Twitter @BFishLifeCoach
Instagram @bethfisherlifecoach
facebook.com/bethfisherlifecoach